An Authentic Guide to Meditation

By
Shar Khentrul Jamphel Lodrö

Edited by
Adrian Hekel

Dzokden

Author: Shar Khentrul Jamphel Lodrö
Editor: Adrian Hekel

First Edition

ISBN: 978-1-958229-08-8 (Paperback)
ISBN: 978-1-958229-09-5 (ePub)

Published by:
DZOKDEN

This work was produced by Dzokden, a non-profit institution operated entirely by volunteers. This organization is dedicated to propagating a non-sectarian view of all the world's spiritual traditions and to teaching Buddhism in a way that is both completely authentic and at the same time practical and accessible to Western culture. It is especially dedicated to spreading the Jonang tradition, a rare gem from a remote part of Tibet that preserves the precious teachings of the Kalachakra.

For more information about scheduled activities or available materials, or if you would like to make a donation, please contact:

Dzokden
3436 Divisadero Street
San Francisco, CA 94123
USA

www.dzokden.org
office@dzokden.org

Contents

Letter from the Author

The meditation instructions presented in this book are not something to be read a few times and then put aside - it can be incredibly valuable to familiarise yourself with them and practise them as a life-long goal. If you are dedicated to putting these instructions into practice, your life will have great meaning and purpose. Just a little practice, however, will not necessarily lead to any attainment unless you have an exceptional degree of innate spiritual ability. Just as an acrobat cannot perform stunts when they are born and needs to practise continuously, meditation is something you need to practise again and again. Usually you will need great perseverance, commitment and wisdom, along with the skillful guidance of teachers or spiritual friends. After a while, however, your practice will become second-nature and not so much effort will be required; it then becomes a source of joy and great meaning.

If you cannot relate ideas such as enlightenment or the jhanas, remember that the essential goal of Buddhist practice is to always be mindful of your conduct and to keep a good heart at all times. From this point of view, meditation is an important method for 'getting used to' the feelings of love and compassion that you should be trying to develop all the time. Whoever you are and whatever you do, this is sure to benefit you greatly.

Shar Khentrul Rinpoche Jamphel Lodrö
Belgrave, Australia

Shakyamuni Buddha meditating under the Bodhi tree

Introduction

Nowadays the practice of meditation is becoming increasingly popular. It is recognised as being an important part of a healthy lifestyle and as an essential aspect of many spiritual traditions. As learning to meditate correctly can potentially lead to so much benefit, I felt a booklet such as this would be helpful in order to present the meditation path in a way that is both authentic and accessible.

Firstly, I believe this material is authentic because it is based on traditional Buddhist teachings which have been tested for over two thousand years - by following these instructions countless meditators have been able to discover the true nature of their reality and have completely transformed their lives. These teachings offer a practical approach which can benefit anyone, regardless of their race or religion. We call them 'Buddhist', however, to declare that they come from an authentic source.

I have tried to make this material accessible, meanwhile, by minimising the use of jargon and referring to a variety of modern-day sources. I have attempted to summarise a variety of meditation methods which not only were effective during the Buddha's time, but have also been used with considerable success by modern-day teachers.

My hope is that this book will guide you to finding a type of meditation that will 'bring you home' whenever you choose – to a space of calm clarity in which you can find peace and restore your energy, or from which you can effectively engage in the world and move gracefully with the waves of life. Yet above all, I hope that this book can serve as a 'bridge' to enlightenment, whether you are following a Buddhist path or any other authentic spiritual tradition. For those who are particularly interested in the Buddhist path, I warmly encourage you to explore the references at the end of this book, especially the *Unveiling Your Sacred Truth* Series.

GOOD LUCK!

CHAPTER 1
The Preliminaries

I. Why is it Important to Meditate?

We all have limitless potential to develop our mind yet currently it is afflicted by dullness, distraction and uncontrolled emotions, as well as the potential for these states to arise. Meditation can purify and refine our mind. On one level, it can help us lead a more effective, balanced, calm and peaceful life. On a deeper level, it can help us develop powerful strength of mind and focus. If we are able to renounce our attachment to worldly interests and develop great compassion, it can lead to the discovery of our enlightened nature.

We must remember that meditation develops the non-physical mind consciousness. Nowadays we are beginning to understand that mental phenomena arise from a hidden dimension of reality that is more fundamental than the split between mind and matter. This is what Buddhists believe to be the *subtle mind,* and many meditators have discovered this directly. Unlike the five sense consciousnesses, which depend on certain physical organs, this subtle mind can be trained in a limitless way. Therefore the practice of meditation can lead to extraordinary results if we persevere with it.

You may ask, how will meditation benefit you in your daily life? Firstly, your quality of life depends on how you perceive and respond to things, and this is determined by the quality of your conscious awareness. Meditation practice can enhance this, so you can learn to approach life from a space of increased calm, clarity, insight and understanding. It can therefore help you feel present, grounded and connected to all of your experiences. Rather than being caught up in reacting to external events, you can be in a better position to understand things as they are and respond in a wise way, with patience and kindness towards yourself and others. You can then discover an inner freedom where you can choose your responses rather than reacting, resisting or seeking distraction.

There are also many health benefits of meditation. They include improved coping skills, memory, efficiency, better sleep, an increased relaxation response, less anxiety and depression, and a lessening of chronic pain (as you can learn to just be aware of pain without buying into it). It can also lead to reduced blood pressure and heart rate, improved immune function and benefits in a wide range of physical conditions, including heart disease, diabetes and cancer.

However, the greatest benefit of authentic meditation practice is that it is a key which opens the door to enlightenment, or developing great wisdom and compassion. This may seem a 'far out' concept, but if you really develop the skill of meditation, you will see life from a whole new perspective and appreciate the precious opportunity that this life gives you to discover the truth of your reality. If you sincerely set foot on this journey, you will no doubt find many other benefits in your life as well.

In this book I shall begin by defining meditation, followed by a brief outline of the meditation path and how to choose a suitable object. Then I will describe the actual method of meditation, beginning by setting up the right outer and inner environment. Then, using mindfulness of breathing as an example, we will journey through the various stages of meditation leading to perfect single-pointed concentration. This is followed by a summary of the hindrances to meditation and their antidotes, followed by instructions on how to engage in analytical meditation and a description of several advanced meditation practices.

II. WHAT IS MEDITATION?

The word 'meditation' is well-known throughout the world. However, its meaning is often limited, misunderstood and presented in a way that is a little simplistic, at least from the point of view of Buddhism. The meaning of meditation is vast like an ocean and encompasses a treasury of skills and methods. It is not necessary to understand its numerous meanings at this stage, yet it is vital to develop the correct view of meditation and comprehend the most fundamental points.

Firstly, the Tibetan word for meditation is *gom*, which means both familiarity with and the process of becoming familiar. From a Buddhist perspective, it means learning to recognise and becoming habituated to a view of reality that reflects the true nature of your experience, and through this you develop wisdom and compassion. As you practise meditation in this way, you become habituated to a truer sense of who you really are and you make this view more solid and stable as your concentration develops. Rather than just being something intellectual, this view can then become part of your living reality.

On a simple level, we can think of meditation as a *tool* for emotional and mental wellbeing, and for achieving balance in our lives. In the modern world we often carry a lot of tension in our bodies, moved by the habit of compulsive thinking and a culture which encourages us to move up and on. Meditation, then, can be a tool to *come down gracefully* and rediscover a balance point where you can choose to be still and restore your energy.

A monk showing the seven-point meditation posture of Vairochana

By finding this balance point you can then be more effective and clear-minded when the time comes to move and act in the world, as in your work and family life. This is like knowing where the beach is and being able to return to it whenever you choose, as you swim in the ocean of life and encounter conditions that are sometimes calm and at other times wild and stormy. You can also imagine a bag that you are carrying by your side. At first it is quite light, yet if you keep on carrying it with the same arm for many hours, it will get heavier and heavier with each passing minute. This is similar to the tension we carry with us - all our stories, fears, worries, stress and responsibilities. Meditation allows you to put the bag down, and you can then pick it up again with much more ease, energy and clarity.

There are two main levels of meditation: *shamatha* (also known as calm abiding) and *vipasyana* (or clear seeing). Shamatha refers to the technique of single-pointed meditation, where you focus intently on a single object in order to 'get used to it' and so unify and concentrate the mind; it therefore becomes much more stable than the normal ordinary mind. It also describes the blissful and undistracted state of mind that is the result of shamatha practice. Vipasyana, meanwhile, refers to insight meditation. This emphasises understanding the true nature of the mind and phenomena.

If we think of a candle, shamatha is like the stability of the flame and vipasyana is like the brightness of the flame. To see a picture clearly you need a flame that is both steady and bright. Similarly, to discover the true nature of your experience you need a mind that is both calm and clear. This does not mean, however, that shamatha and vipasyana are completely separate. Many teachers liken these two methods to two ends of a stick or two sides of a hand. The more calm and concentration you develop, the more likely you are to develop insight. The more insight you develop, the easier it is for your mind to be focused and calm. In order to completely eradicate harmful emotions and mental states, however, it is necessary for both to be present. This is known as the *union* of shamatha and vipasyana.

All types of meditation follow the same basic method:

1. Calm your body;
2. Focus on your chosen object;
3. When thoughts or feelings come, just watch and be aware of them; and
4. Bring your mind gently back to the object.

Shamatha meditation emphasises the second step, as you train yourself to become so habituated to a stable mind or so familiar with an object that distracting thoughts become very subtle and eventually no longer arise. Insight meditation mainly emphasises the third step, as you learn to follow thoughts and feelings with full awareness or examine their nature. With either method it is crucial that you do not try to 'block' thoughts or feelings, but rather be aware of them and gently bring your mind back to the object of meditation.

These four steps also contain three key skills which you progressively develop as you learn to meditate. The first is *relaxation*, where the body learns to let go of all its habitual tension and feel 'spacious'. The second is *mindfulness*, the absorption of the mind into the object of meditation, so the mind becomes 'full' of the object. The final skill is *awareness* or *vigilance*, which refers to an aspect of the mind which acts as a vigilant guard, checking to see whether you are mindful or not and making the object more and more vivid. It also alerts you if you are falling into states of dullness, agitation or other hindrances, and maintains a receptive awareness of objects in the background such as sights and sounds. These three qualities are like the roots, trunk and foliage of a tree. As our practice grows, the roots of relaxation go deeper, the trunk of mindfulness gets stronger and the foliage of vigilance reaches higher.

The three key meditation skills: relaxation, mindfulness and awareness or vigilance

III. OVERVIEW OF THE MEDITATION PATH

Taking up a meditation practice begins when you clarify your motivation and gain a philosophical understanding of where this practice can lead you. It is also helpful to establish a strong foundation of morality, discipline and balance in your life. For some people this may mean simplifying life to make space for meditation practice and for others this may mean becoming more actively involved in life. For others still it may mean entering a monastery or making the choice to adhere to a particular set of precepts. This foundation of discipline helps you develop mindfulness as you go about your daily life. The motivation with which you engage in meditation practice may be to benefit yourself in this life, to attain liberation from suffering or to achieve complete enlightenment for the benefit of all beings. Each motivation is equally valid and we cannot say one is better than the others, yet a vaster motivation is likely to lead to more benefit.

In general, you begin by choosing an appropriate meditation object (whether this be one or several) and engage in single-pointed meditation in order to attain *shamatha mind*. You progress gradually through nine attentional states or stages, leading to a stable state of peace and perfect concentration which can be directed upon any object you choose. Those who attain shamatha will be free from emotions, and are able to remain in a peaceful state of mind for a great length of time. This meditation is common to both Buddhist and non-Buddhist traditions. If you make some degree of progress towards attaining single-pointed concentration you will discover states of great peace during meditation and notice many benefits in your daily life.

If you are not attached to this peaceful state of mind and have the courage and diligence to progress further, you will reach a stage where you are highly motivated to keep practising, inspired by many blissful and peaceful experiences. This can lead to the attainment of extremely refined states of concentration known as the *jhanas*. These are incredibly blissful, fully absorbed states of mind during which you are completely unaware of any external reality.

The result of shamatha or jhana practice can be a worldly or 'samsaric' attainment, meaning it may not ultimately lead to freedom from suffering. Alternatively, at least from a Buddhist point of view, with the right motivation and wisdom this attainment can be directed towards enlightenment. From this perspective shamatha is not the ultimate goal but rather a fundamental step towards discovering true insight into the nature of your experience. It is then actually possible to overcome all destructive emotions and mental states, achieving perfect and lasting freedom from the experience of suffering.

Some people develop the calm mind of shamatha first followed by insight while others develop insight first and then later develop meditative stability. Others, meanwhile, develop calm and insight at the same time, or in tandem, while in others it takes a great deal of perseverance to be able to settle the mind and cultivate the path.

IV. Choosing a Meditation Object

In order to find a meditation path that is most suitable for you, it is crucial to find one or more meditation objects which suit your personality type. Ideally it is an object that you will fall in love with. You can choose this object based on your experience or preference, or a teacher can recommend one to you. A particular object is usually chosen to help you overcome a particular weakness or because it builds on your strengths. For example, if you have a short temper, contemplation of loving kindness may be a very suitable object as it serves as an antidote for anger. If you have a *feeling* personality-type, you may be drawn to loving kindness or devotional practices for a different reason, as this kind of object would suit your personality. Similarly, *thinking-types* may be drawn to certain forms of analytical meditation and *sensing-types* may benefit from techniques which emphasise mindfulness of the body or sensory awareness.

Another consideration is that when you are meditating to achieve single-pointed concentration, as your focus improves you can choose an object that is more and more subtle. At the beginning a moving object such as slow walking or breathing may be most suitable, yet at a certain point it is better to concentrate on a stable, non-moving object such as a holy image or a visualised mental object.

According to Mahayana and Vajrayana Buddhism, there are an infinite number of meditation objects to suit different types of beings in order to develop single-pointed concentration. The Theravada teachings, meanwhile, describe forty different objects of contemplation to suit people with different temperaments.

We can divide almost all meditation objects into eight categories:

1. Breathing meditations (spontaneous breathing and controlled breathing).
2. Visualisations (such as an image of the Buddha or visual objects called *kasinas* which represent the four elements and four colours).
3. Mantra meditations (where a sound or group of syllables is repeated, often together with a visualisation).
4. Movement meditations (such as slow walking or yoga).

5. Meditation on energy centers or chakras.

6. Jhana meditations (very deep states of meditative absorption).

7. Analytical meditations (including contemplations such as impermanence, loving kindness or prayers and devotional practices, as well as questioning the true nature of reality).

8. Open awareness meditations (including open awareness of the contents of mind or the dark room practice from the Kalachakra Tantra)

The first six categories emphasise the development of single-pointed concentration while the final two categories emphasise insight; however each category can lead to both concentration and insight. The Kalachakra dark room practice, for example, is used to attain shamatha by focusing on the non-conceptual state, and at a certain stage this leads to direct insight into the true nature of reality.

If your mind is afflicted predominantly with excessive thoughts or you have a 'speculative temperament', which is quite common with our busy and tense lifestyles, focusing on the natural flow of the breath can be an effective way to make the mind still and relax the body. Awareness of internal feelings and sensations can also help achieve a more relaxed state, as can mindfulness of body movement as in slow walking or yoga. For walking meditation, you should focus intently on each moment of the movement of each foot, and you may like to synchronise this with the breath ('breathing in aware of the left foot, breathing out aware of the right foot') or perhaps a mantra (*bud-dho* is used in the Thai tradition, with one syllable recited quietly with each step). The use of the breath as a meditation object is described at great length later in this book.

Walking meditation focuses on awareness of the ground

If your predominant afflictive emotion is hatred or anger, then loving kindness, also called *metta*, may be a good object to meditate upon. Similarly, meditation on empathetic joy may be a suitable object if you have a tendency towards jealousy. To meditate on loving kindness, you should recognise that all beings are seeking happiness, just like yourself, and cultivate the wish that others find genuine happiness and its causes. This meditation is the basis for more advanced contemplations on love and compassion presented in the Mahayana Buddhist tradition..

If, on the other hand, attachment or lust is your predominant affliction, an effective method is to bring to mind a desirable person and think of all the unattractive features of the body such as flesh, bones, internal organs, pus, blood and urine. You can also recollect the different stages of decay of a human corpse, which the Theravada teachings describe in nine stages known as the *nine charnel ground contemplations*. Although this may sound repulsive, those who carry out this form of meditation are often surprised that their experience is quite blissful, since bliss naturally emerges once afflictive desire is removed.

Suitable objects for those who have a faithful nature (feeling-types) include recollection of the Buddha and the Three Jewels, deities and virtues such as generosity. This may especially apply to those with a background in Christianity or other faith-based religions who are drawn to prayer or devotional practices. On the other hand, for those who are thinking-types, suitable objects include mindfulness of death and impermanence, contemplation of the body as a collection of elements and contemplation of interdependence. These contemplations can also be an antidote for pride or arrogance.

One effective visualisation method, which combines several of these objects, is to become aware that your body has originated from afflictions and karmic propensities and then visualise it as an impure collection of flesh, bones, blood, pus, excrement and any other characteristics you can think of. At the centre of the heart visualise a luminous light symbolising your enlightened nature slowly radiating throughout the body. The mind remains in single-pointed concentration following the light without distraction and your entire body becomes indestructible luminous light. This symbolises complete purification and gradual attainment of your enlightened nature.

So long as your motivation is pure and your view is correct, tantric meditations involving visualisations and mantras can be a very effective way to practice. These may especially suit those with an *intuitive* personality-type. Meditations which involve visualisation and mantra (known as *deity yoga* or the *generation stage*) can connect you to an aspect of your enlightened nature, and a particular deity may suit a particular temperament. For example, the Manjushri mantra OM AH RA PA DZA NA DHI can be used to develop wisdom and the Chenrezig mantra OM MA NI PADME HUNG can be used to evoke compassion. The Vajrapani mantra, HUNG VAJRA PHET, can help you generate compassionate power and strength. The Medicine Buddha mantra, meanwhile, can assist you to heal yourself so you can benefit others: TAYATA OM BEKANZE BEKANZE MAHA BEKANZE RADZA SAMUDGATE SVAHA. Finally, the White Tara mantra OM TARE TUTARE TURE SVAHA can connect you with the feminine quality of love and long life. Each of these practices is associated with a specific visualisation, details of which can be found in various texts. Anyone with the right motivation can receive some benefit from reciting these mantras; however, they are more powerful if you have received an initiation or have undertaken specific study.

Energy centers or *chakras* are another meditation object, though generally in Buddhism they are part of quite advanced practices which usually require certain preliminaries to be completed (known as the *completion stage*). Performing these practices as a beginner is like building a house without a solid foundation and is unlikely to lead to much benefit. Several non-Buddhist yogic schools offer powerful methods to activate the chakras and can be very effective for certain types of people. However, if you are aiming for enlightenment, you must carefully investigate whether there are differences between the Buddhist and yogic views, and ask yourself which path will benefit you most in the long term.

A final consideration is to choose a meditation object (or objects) which helps you develop concentration in such a way that you can integrate this into your daily life experience. Mindfulness of the present moment or open awareness can therefore be a very practical method, as your experience in life will mirror your experience in meditation. Your daily work can also become a form of meditation – often you will find yourself in a state of 'flow' when your work is neither too boring (leading to dullness) or too challenging (leading to stress and agitation). In fact the Buddha once told an old woman who wanted to meditate to remain aware of every movement of her hands as she drew water from a well, and this became her daily practice.

You will also notice various cycles throughout the day when some meditation objects may be more suitable that others. If you attend closely to the body's natural cycles you will find that the mind and body alternates between periods of movement (or expending energy) and stillness (restoring energy). During periods of movement it is more effective to use a meditation object in which our minds are 'directed' or channeled into a clear direction, such as an analytical meditation, mantra or counting the breath.

In periods of stillness, you might favour more 'receptive' meditations, as the mind is naturally more calm, open and blissful. You can even learn to meditate during the states of dreaming and deep sleep, and this can lead to being able to maintain a continuous awareness, day and night.

V. CREATING THE RIGHT ENVIRONMENT

For a seed to grow into a tree, we need various conditions such as fertile soil, sunlight and rain. Similarly, in order to train the mind in meditation we need various outer and inner conditions. This includes the right location, the right posture, the right state of mind or intention and preliminary practices to calm the mind.

(i) The Right Location

Firstly it is helpful to prepare a location that is conducive to meditation practice: quiet, clean, free from clutter, blessed and free from interruptions or distractions. Certain locations suit different types of practice – a peaceful forest environment, for example, can help with the development of calm and concentration, while a place with a vast open view can be an effective place to cultivate insight. Although an environment which is noisy or contains many distractions may be a hindrance for beginners, if you can develop a good meditation practice in spite of such challenges this may actually lead to greater accomplishment.

When beginning to meditate, it is best to keep to a strict schedule and hold the sessions at the same place, focusing on the same object. The amount of time you spend in meditation, during each practice, depends on your ability and frame of mind. Five to fifteen minutes a session is a good place to start, and several times each day is ideal.

(ii) The Right Posture

It is also important to know the elements of the posture which are most conducive to a stable mind, because the coarse mind is temporarily associated with and influenced by the body while you are alive. Mental development, too, is temporarily associated with the body until you leave it behind at the moment of death. In all Buddhist practices, material things are regarded as a useful means to an end during this temporary lifetime. The body, in this way, is like a boat and the meditator is like a passenger. The passenger is dependent on the boat while crossing the ocean and without the boat the passenger could drown or fail to reach land. Yet once the destination is reached, the boat is no longer useful.

You can meditate while sitting, lying down, walking or standing—and each of these postures can be used formally or informally.

For sitting, you should use a comfortable straight-backed padded chair or a meditation stool or cushion. The hands rest together either in the lap or on the thighs, while the back is straight like an arrow and the chin is slightly tucked in. For lying down, if your mind is agitated you can lie on your back with your arms by your side and hands open (though you should avoid this posture if your mind is dull). To support a greater clarity of mind, you can lie on the right side with your right hand underneath your face, legs together with the knees slightly bent and your left arm down the left side of your body. For walking and standing, you should hold your hands, right in left, in front of your body, or you can interlace your fingers if you find this difficult. Being sure to have an upright but relaxed posture, you should let your arms hang naturally.

It is useful to know in detail the elements of the sitting posture as this is the posture most conducive to effective meditation, which is necessary if you are determined to achieve high states of concentration. It consists of seven features and is known as the seven-point posture of Buddha Vairochana. These seven features include:

1. *Legs (crossed)*

Ideally the legs should be crossed in the *vajra posture*, with the left foot resting on the right thigh and the right foot on the left thigh. If this position is too difficult, any comfortable cross-legged posture will do, though note that more stability and collectedness is achieved if the buttocks are raised so that the hips tilt forwards. As our bodies are very sensitive to our environment, by sitting on the ground you can gain a sense of the great energy associated with the immense earth beneath you, supporting or holding you. A good cross-legged position provides excellent physical balance and also represents a balance or union of method and wisdom.

Equally important to sitting in the appropriate position is to be comfortable. The optimal sitting posture contributes to the development of your meditation but sitting comfortably means that you will be less distracted in your meditation and you will find it much easier for your body to relax. Therefore you may choose to sit on a chair with your legs relaxed, knees at right angles and buttocks firmly supported by the chair, remembering to keep your back straight.

2. *Hands (in the lap)*

The right hand should be placed on top of the left hand palm up, gently resting in the lap (for female meditators placing the left hand on top of the right may be more effective). The tips of the thumbs should touch slightly below the navel. The position of the hands expresses the unification of method and wisdom during your practice. You should feel a sense of relaxation from your shoulders to your wrists and down to your hands, allowing any tension in your upper body to be released.

3. *Back (spine straight)*

The body should be held upright like an arrow or pile of golden coins, not leaning sideways, backward or forward. This has an enormous effect on the inner winds, which are the subtle movements of energy that circulate within the body and mind, closely related to the breath and capable of being used with great effect in certain advanced practices. The straight back also helps your mind stay alert and attentive. You should try to feel balanced and clear on the inside of your body from the top of your head to your base. You can make slight adjustments throughout the meditation to ensure your posture is balanced and straight. The goal is to remain still, relaxed and alert; being stiff and immobile is a hindrance to awareness.

4. *Shoulders and elbows (drawn back and slightly away from the body)*

The shoulders and arms should be drawn back a little and slightly curved so they are evenly placed on either side of the body, which helps the lungs to expand correctly and aids breathing during meditation. The elbows should remain a little away from the body.

5. *Head and neck (chin slightly lowered)*

The head should not be too high and not bent down too much either. Keep the head straight and centered, with the chin slightly tucked in and the nose held in line with the navel. Try not to bend the neck sideways or backwards.

6. *Mouth (face relaxed and tip of the tongue touching the upper palate)*

The teeth and lips should be held in a natural position with the teeth barely touching. It is important to keep the face and jaw relaxed and peaceful, which will prevent excessive swallowing. The tip of the tongue should be gently placed behind the upper teeth, helping to sharpen the mind and preventing dryness and dribbling. If your mind is quite agitated and you find it difficult to achieve a calm state, placing the tongue behind the bottom teeth may help loosen and calm the mind.

7. *Eyes (gazing past the tip of the nose)*

The eyes should not be opened too wide, nor should they be completely closed. If they are too widely opened you may become easily distracted, and if completely closed your mind may become foggy or dull. When beginning, however, keeping the eyes softly closed may help your body enter into a deeper state of relaxation. After meditating like this for a little while you will find you naturally become more balanced and may want to open the eyes slightly. Also, when a visualised object is used as a focus for meditation, or when the mind is too agitated, it is important to close your eyes.

There are different methods of directing your gaze. The first method is to gaze directly in front of you at any colour that is not too bright, or a pleasant or holy object such as a flower or an image of the Buddha. The second (and more common) method is to direct the eyes downwards, gently and serenely gazing into the space a little in front of the tip of your nose. Do not focus too strongly, keep your eyes still and allow natural blinking to occur. These two methods are suitable for beginners. Other specific meditation methods involve gazing upward with wide open eyes into expansive space, which may in fact naturally happen when the mind has reached a certain level of calm and clear insight begins to arise. Another method, practiced widely in the Jonang tradition of Tibetan Buddhism, is to meditate in a completely dark room, eyes wide open and gazing upwards, focused about twelve inches in front of your forehead into the all-embracing darkness.

Anyone who perseveres with practising this posture correctly, regardless of how hard or painful it may initially seem, will eventually find it extremely comfortable and beneficial for health. The main benefit, however, is that it will assist your meditation practice and mental development in the long-term. If you are not really concerned about practising intensively and attaining shamatha, it may be just as effective to practise in any position that you find comfortable and easy to relax in.

(iii) The Right Attitude

There are many 'inner conditions' which are necessary for successful meditation practice. According to the Theravada teachings, renunciation is the most important condition – this means recognising the truth of suffering and viewing meditation as a tool to overcome your experience of suffering. Some people take up meditation with this in mind, yet forget this intention and become complacent when their practice is going well or their lives have improved. The Buddha likened this to someone who is seeking heartwood but instead cuts off branches or bark from a tree and takes it away, thinking this is heartwood.

In the Tibetan tradition, the ninth Karmapa describes four conditions necessary for successful meditation - renunciation, reliance on a qualified Dharma teacher, a non-sectarian outlook and a mind that is free from expectations. If you are following a Mahayana path, it is important to view the enlightenment of others as more important than your own liberation, recalling the special motivation of bodhicitta and invoking the support of the Buddha or your Dharma teacher. You should also rekindle this motivation at the end of your practice, dedicating it towards the enlightenment of all beings. This ensures that the merit of your practice is secure and can increase; otherwise it can be reduced or destroyed by negativity.

In a practical sense, you should consider yourself a person with 'no history', abandoning concern for memories of the past or future as well as present distractions and expectations. In particular, you should abandon thoughts of discouragement if your practice is not going well, and avoid being carried away by pride and excitement if you encounter good experiences during meditation.

(iv) Preliminary Practices

In order to begin meditation with a mind that is calm and receptive, it is useful to carry out a few preliminary practices which can help you achieve this.

The first of these is a brief practice from the Tibetan tradition called *exhaling the foul air*, which involves visualising all your impurities being forcefully blown out through your nostrils. This helps remove counterproductive currents of energy from the subtle body which are associated with attachment, aversion and ignorance. As the breath and the mind are intimately connected, this practice is an excellent starting point for any meditation.

A simple version of this practice is to take three deep breaths, each time inhaling to the pit of the stomach and holding it for a while, then forcefully exhaling through both nostrils while visualising all impure energies such as lust and hatred leaving your mind and body. This can be repeated any time during your meditation if you feel you are losing focus.

A slightly more elaborate version involves a total of nine breaths. First, inhale deeply through the right nostril while pressing the left nostril closed with your left thumb. You may like to steady the position of your left hand by holding the left index finger at the center of the forehead. Then press your right nostril closed with your left middle finger and release the left nostril, exhaling through the left nostril. Repeat this three times, and then inhale deeply through the left nostril while continuing to press the right nostril closed with your left middle finger; then press your left nostril closed with your left thumb and release the right nostril, exhaling through the right nostril. Repeat this three times. Finally, put your hands back on your lap and inhale deeply through both nostrils, and then exhale through both nostrils. Again repeat this three times, making a total of nine breaths.

After this breathing practice, a useful ritual to follow is to rock your body from side to side and then be aware of contact points and the sounds around you. First check that your spine is straight and gently rock your body from side to side, with movements becoming smaller and smaller until you naturally come to a balance point. Then be aware of the contact points between your legs or feet and the floor, your buttocks and your seat and your hands and your lap, and then quickly make sure that your belly, shoulders, tongue and jaw are all relaxed. Finally become aware of all the sounds around you – in front of you, behind you and to both sides – simply being receptive and just listening without any reaction. Now you are ready to meditate.

CHAPTER 2

The Breath as an Object and the Stages of Meditation

I will now describe how to use the breath as an object of meditation, and how this can gradually lead to the attainment of shamatha. As many people in the modern world live in a very busy, stimulating environment, excessive thinking and agitation are the primary afflictions we need to overcome. This is often related to a great deal of 'nervous tension' carried in our bodies. Breathing meditation is an excellent method to counter these afflictions, and was also the most widely taught meditation method by the Buddha.

Using breathing meditation as a template, I will now describe four progressive stages: mindfulness of the present moment, getting the mind on the object, keeping the mind on the object and fine tuning the mind (leading to shamatha). This presentation covers the *nine progressive attentional states* in the Tibetan tradition, based on the teachings of Buddha Maitreya and Kamalashila, as well as the stages of breathing meditation presented in the *Anapanasati Sutta* in the Theravada tradition. In the first two stages relaxation is emphasised, while in the third stage mindfulness or stability of attention is emphasised. Having achieved good relaxation and stability, vigilance or vividness of attention is then emphasised in the later stages.

You have 'reached' a particular stage when your experience in meditation matches the description of the stage for most of the

Take the breath as an object of meditation

meditation, in *all* of your sessions. Nevertheless, the stage you have reached can appear to vary considerably from one sitting to the next, so it is important to adjust your method to suit your state of mind. If, for example, your mind is much more agitated than usual, it is a good idea to start from the beginning, first establishing relaxed mindfulness of the body, feelings and mind anchored by the breath. Generally you can progress quickly through the initial stages before reaching your 'usual stage', as long as you remember not to rush ahead too quickly. 'Careful patience' is the surest way to progress.

Remember also that your meditation path is never fixed, and at a certain stage you may decide that a different object or meditation method is more beneficial. For example, when you reach a certain level of concentration you might prefer to meditate with open awareness as an object, use a visualisation and mantra or perhaps spend more time on study and analytical meditation. Whatever object you choose, however, the stages leading to shamatha still apply to your meditation practice.

I. Mindfulness of the Present Moment with the Breath

Many people find it difficult to settle on a single meditation object right away. The aim of this first stage, then, is to create a receptive (but not reactive) frame of mind, able to simply note all external stimuli without reacting to them or taking them up. In addition, you can use the breath to anchor your awareness and consciously relax the body. You can therefore quickly generate a state of mind which is both calm and alert, not too tight and not too loose.

What is Mindfulness?

Literally this means the mind is 'full' of whatever it is experiencing. It is when you just notice your experience and simply remain present with what is, without thinking about or describing what is happening. One Theravada teacher described mindfulness in terms of five characteristics:

1. A *central present* awareness.
2. A *holding* and *giving* of attention, either with an open receptive focus or a more collected focus.
3. An awareness which is *non-judgmental*, stepping back rather than being caught up in judgment, seeing things as they are and not as we are.
4. A *receptive* quality, open to a full range of experience without resisting or reacting, like a satellite dish receiving information.
5. A *non-personal* awareness, not buying into or taking personally whatever is noted or known, including all painful thoughts, feelings and sensations.

In order to develop mindfulness, you first need to be aware of the different elements which make up your experience. This is described at length in a teaching known as the four foundations of mindfulness, from the *Satipatthana Sutta*. This includes:

1. Mindfulness of the body

This includes mindfulness of breathing, knowing when you are experiencing a long or a short breath, being aware of the movement of breath and the calmness this brings though the whole body. It also includes: mindfulness of body position (knowing when you are walking, standing, sitting or lying), mindfulness of where you are going, mindfulness of how you are moving, eating, drinking and defecating, mindfulness when talking and keeping silent, mindfulness of the unattractive features of your body, mindfulness of the elements which make up your body and mindfulness of death and impermanence.

2. *Mindfulness of feelings*

This includes simply knowing when you are experiencing a pleasant feeling, a painful feeling or a neutral feeling. This can come about either through contact with the five senses or through contact with mental objects, including perceptions, memories, thoughts and mental images. More subtle feelings may also arise when your mind is calm, such as a sense of bliss or happiness pervading your body.

3. *Mindfulness of states of mind*

This includes knowing that a mind with desire is a mind with desire, while a mind without desire is a mind without desire. Similarly, you know when anger, ignorance, contraction, distraction and other states are present, and you know when these states are absent. You also know when the mind is concentrated and when it is liberated, and when this is not the case.

4. *Mindfulness of phenomena*

This means you are mindful of all phenomena or contents of the mind. It can include awareness of sensory objects such as sounds, visual objects, tastes, smells and tactile sensations, as well as mental objects such as memories and thought proliferations. However, it also refers to knowing that the nature of such phenomena is impermanent, suffering (or uncontrollable) and devoid of self-nature.

In summary, mindfulness means being aware of a full range of experiences, beginning with awareness of the body and extending to feelings, mental states, sensory objects and mental objects. You can then discover that your mind can feel 'full' rather than fragmented, disembodied or caught up in thinking. The *Satipatthana Sutta* also states that you should contemplate all of these objects as 'arising, passing away and both arising and passing away', as well as 'internally, externally and both internally and externally'. This can give added depth to your practice of mindfulness, helping you extend it to the outside world and align your experience with the Buddhist view of reality.

Mindfulness using the Breath as an Anchor

Although it is possible to practise mindfulness by simply paying attention to whatever arises in your experience, it can be even more helpful to anchor this experience with awareness of the breath. The Buddha thus taught the *Anapanasati Sutta* in order to show how mindfulness of breathing could fulfill the four foundations of mindfulness, and how this could lead to liberation.

This sutta gives instructions for *sixteen mindfulness breaths*, which is a quick and effective method to calm the mind down and at the same time gain clear awareness of our experience. These sixteen breaths also refer to sixteen stages of concentration which are accomplished in sequence; however, here we consider them together.

To begin this practice you should find a quiet place and establish the correct posture, with body straightened, and be mindful as you naturally breathe in and breathe out. You should say to yourself or simply know:

Breathing in long (I am) aware of the long (or short) breath,
*   breathing out (I am) aware of the long (or short) breath*
Breathing in short aware of the short breath,
*   breathing out aware of the short breath*
Breathing in aware of the body,
*   breathing out aware of the body*
Breathing in calming the body,
*   breathing out calming the body*
Breathing in aware of the feelings,
*   breathing out aware of the feelings*
Breathing in calming the feelings,
*   breathing out calming the feelings*
Breathing in aware of joy,
*   breathing out aware of joy*
Breathing in aware of happiness,
*   breathing out aware of happiness*
Breathing in aware of the mind,
*   breathing out aware of the mind*
Breathing in gladdening the mind,
*   breathing out gladdening the mind*
Breathing in concentrating the mind,
*   breathing out concentrating the mind*
Breathing in liberating the mind,
*   breathing out liberating the mind*
Breathing in aware of impermanence,
*   breathing out aware of impermanence*
Breathing in aware of fading away,
*   breathing out aware of fading away*
Breathing in aware of liberation,
*   breathing out aware of liberation*

Breathing in letting go,
   breathing out letting go

Repeat this cycle of breathing again and again, noticing how your mind and body become calm, clear and present. At first it is helpful to repeat the instructions silently to yourself as you are breathing in and out and contemplate each topic while you are doing this, especially impermanence. You can think, for example, how there is no permanent self in your body, feelings or mind, how each of these has a 'suffering' or uncontrollable nature and how there is no 'self' which controls what happens. Eventually you can let go of this and 'just know' that you are mindful of all of these various elements while you are breathing, entering a more receptive state of awareness. Then when your mind starts to wander or loses interest you can return to silently repeating the instructions, perhaps in a condensed way using two, four or eight mindfulness breaths. By alternating in this way you should be able to maintain good concentration with some practice.

The breath as an 'anchor' for mindfulness is something you can always come back to if you are having difficulty in meditation or in daily life. It is like the beach. Challenging situations which emerge in meditation or in life are like waves in the ocean, yet if you know how to return to the beach, you will avoid being carried out to sea or being dumped by large waves. You can easily return to this practice in daily life, as you are breathing all the time and you are learning to associate mindfulness with the breath. During breaks in your normal activity, you can take a few deep breaths and consciously bring yourself to the relaxed, alert state you have developed during formal meditation.

II. Getting the Mind on the Meditation Object (Like a Waterfall Cascading over Rocks)

By first cultivating mindfulness of the present moment, you will discover how an alert mind can co-exist with a relaxed body. Then, in order to develop a more focused type of concentration, you can focus on a narrower field of attention. If you were to focus on a single object to begin with, you are very likely to constrict your mind and body, aggravating any pre-existing tension. This is especially true in the modern world where people often have a great deal of tension stored in their bodies.

According to the *Anapanasati Sutta*, the most effective way to begin this practice is to simply observe the breath enough to know whether it is long or short. You therefore say to yourself:

Breathing in (I am) aware of the short (or long) breath,
breathing out aware of the short (or long) breath.
Breathing in aware of the long (or short) breath,
breathing out aware of the long (or short) breath.

The key to meditation at this stage is to maintain a relaxed state of mind and the biggest obstacle you will face is the tendency for your mind to *control* the breath. This instruction therefore allows you to maintain close awareness of the natural flow of the breath, yet at the same time resist controlling it. Letting go of the tendency to control your breath (by just noticing when it stops of its own accord) helps you relax while directing your attention to the length of the breath heightens your alertness.

The sutta does not specify where we should focus on the breath. To achieve relaxation it is beneficial to be aware of the breath through the whole body, yet you may find it more natural to focus on a specific area such as the chest or belly. As you become aware of the whole body 'breathing', your perception of the breath becomes more subtle. This is known as the inner wind, which sometimes feels like energy currents traveling throughout the body. You can visualise this subtle breath circulating around your body, going through each part in turn, or you can imagine that your whole body is exhaling and inhaling, as if a wave of breath was traveling through your body. You can also help your body relax by placing the tongue behind the bottom teeth and slowing down the out-breath. If these methods fail to calm your mind, however, it may be that there is an area of tension in a particular part of your body, perhaps linked to certain painful emotions – in this case it can help to focus your breath specifically upon this area, observing anything that comes up and expanding the breath around this area.

Another technique at this stage is to count the breath, with one count per each respiration. One method is to repeat 'one, one, one...' throughout one inhalation and exhalation, and then 'two, two, two...' for the duration of the next breath, repeating this for a total of ten breaths before counting backwards from ten to one. An alternative method is to count 'one' after the inhalation has ceased, followed by 'two' after the exhalation has gone out, again repeating this up to ten times. A further method, used in the Thai tradition, is to recite the mantra *Buddho* with the breath: *Bud* with the in-breath and *Dho* with the out-breath.

This stage of breath meditation roughly equates to the first two attentional states in the Tibetan system, where the focus is on understanding the meditation instructions and achieving a relaxed state:

1. *Placing the Mind on an Object*

    In the beginning, keeping the mind fixed on the object requires much effort. Your ability to stay fixed on the object is initially quite limited and there will only be brief moments when you can do so. It may seem that your mind is even more disturbed than before you started and you get the sense that your discursive thoughts are increasing. However, this is likely to mean you are becoming aware of the usual condition of the mind for the first time, which is the first achievement.

    This first stage is attained through the *power of hearing* or listening to the teacher's instructions on the method of meditation and which object to choose. It is achieved when you can place the mind on the desired object of meditation for even a second or two. If your object is the breath this may be achieved on your first attempt, though if it is a complex visualisation this may take several weeks to accomplish.

2. *Continuous placement*

    The periods of distraction are still longer than the periods of concentration, but the periods during which you are able to stay fixed on the object become more frequent. The mind is becoming more stable and you can occasionally maintain an uninterrupted focus for about one to five minutes, and you get the sense that discursive thoughts are decreasing. This stage is achieved through the *power of reflection*. You are able to fix the mind on the object but still need to recall the instructions over and over again with understanding.

    These first two levels are aimed at getting the mind on an object, and therefore a tightly focused engagement is necessary. The later stages, on the other hand, are aimed at keeping the mind there. The main faults to overcome at these two levels are laziness, especially failing to listen carefully to the instructions, and forgetting the meditation object.

At this stage the movement of thoughts through the mind is likened to a waterfall cascading over rocks; this does not mean that the quantity of our thoughts is increasing, but rather that we are becoming aware of them for the first time.

III. Keeping the Mind on the Meditation Object (Becoming like a River Flowing through a Gorge)

In the previous stage you begin to experience continuous focus upon the breath, directing your attention to awareness of its length or counting the breath while the body becomes more and more relaxed. Once you develop some stability with this method you can simply let your attention flow with the breath, following it through its entire length. You therefore let your mind be absorbed in the breath from the first moment of the in-breath to the last moment, noticing the gap in between, and then following the out-breath from beginning to end. In this way, with your body already quite relaxed, you begin to develop continuous mindfulness and then vigilance. According to the sutta, you should simply know:

Breathing in (I am) aware of the whole body (of the breath),
breathing out aware of the whole body (of the breath).

This instruction is usually taken to refer to the length of the breath, though some interpret it to mean that you should be aware of the breath moving through your entire body. As in the previous stage, you should focus on the breath wherever it comes naturally, moving your focus lower if you need to relax more (for example at the belly) and moving it higher if you need to enhance your vigilance (for example at the tip of the nose). At the same time, however, you should maintain a peripheral awareness of the whole body while you are breathing.

The goal of this stage is to become so absorbed in the breath that you will not be distracted by sounds, sights or even uncomfortable sensations in the body. Especially if you are tired, the mind may become cloudy. At this point vigilant effort is required to tighten up your focus and clearly capture every instant of the breath.

The corresponding attentional states, which aim at establishing mindfulness and then vigilance, are as follows:

3. *Patched placement*

At this stage you become aware of any distractions to your concentration and have developed the ability to bring the mind back to the object of meditation with effort through the *power of mindfulness.* You are able to bring your attention back to the object as soon as it has wandered, as if putting a patch on a cloth. In this way you reset your concentration and are able to remain uninterruptedly focused, generally for about five to ten minutes. You therefore begin to become mindful and progress towards real meditation, as your attention is fixed on the object most of the time in virtually all of your meditation sessions.

Arriving even at this third stage is a big achievement and can make a big difference to your ability to control the mind in everyday life.

4. *Close placement*

Your focus is so strong at this stage that the mind never completely loses fixation upon the object, and coarse agitation is no longer an obstacle. The mind therefore withdraws from a broad range of things to a more narrow focus. You are able to hold the object continuously, but there is still the need to develop increasing levels of clarity or intensity and also to deal with subtle agitation, which is when part of your mind strays from the object of concentration but you do not lose it completely. During this fourth stage the *power of mindfulness* is achieved, so you can hold the object of concentration with such stability that you easily return to it whenever you are distracted. However, you need to make sure that this stability does not come at the expense of relaxation. Therefore you may still need to apply techniques to relax the mind in order to deal with subtle agitation, such as keeping the tongue behind the bottom teeth.

5. *Disciplining the mind*

We have now developed the capacity to overcome coarse dullness and agitation, and the watchfulness or *vigilance* of the mind is developing. The obstacle to overcome at this stage is subtle dullness or sinking, which arises because the withdrawal of the mind from extraneous objects has proceeded too far. This requires much discipline and effort to overcome. There is significant danger of failing to recognise subtle dullness or sinking, which masquerades as a stable and peaceful state of mind, and you need to remove this obstacle by tightening your awareness with increasing vigilance. It can be challenging, however, to overcome subtle dullness without undermining stability, and this can sometimes be quite a delicate balancing act. At this stage we need to generate an uplifted mind through inspiration, for instance by recollecting to the good qualities of shamatha or the Buddha's teachings. It can also help to lift the meditation object and make it smaller or sharper, and to ensure that the tongue now rests behind the top teeth.

At this stage involuntary thoughts continue to arise, though now instead of a waterfall they flow like a river moving smoothly through a gorge. There is still a little resistance to practising, though the results of our efforts are usually quite apparent.

IV. Fine Tuning the Mind (Like a River Flowing Slowly through a Valley)

Having achieved continuous mindfulness of the breath with a high level of discipline, you then need to calm it down. If you jump to this step too soon you may fall prey to dullness and drowsiness. Therefore you must ensure that you complete the previous stage, capturing the whole breath, before you can try to calm it down, just as you must first capture a wild horse before you can tame it.

The sutta therefore gives the instruction:

Breathing in (I am) calming the body (of the breath),
    breathing out calming the body (of the breath).

Difficulty may arise here because we have used substantial willpower to accomplish the previous stage, while now what is required is gentle and persistent letting go. This can be a fine balancing act, and it may help to lower the breath and place more emphasis again on relaxing the body.

The sutta then continues:

Breathing in aware of joy,
    breathing out aware of joy

Breathing in aware of happiness,
  breathing out aware of happiness

This refers to the emergence of joy and happiness (*piti* and *sukha* in Pali) as the breath calms down, like the golden light of dawn emerging on the eastern horizon. You now develop fully sustained attention of the 'beautiful breath' and only traces of discursive thought remain. When you can remain with this object with ease for a long time and a great amount of joy and happiness is experienced, the mind becomes very concentrated and you are able to move on to the next step.

The next stage, according to the sutta, is:

Breathing in aware of the mind,
  breathing out aware of the mind

At this stage your attention is so refined that the breath appears to completely disappear, and is replaced by a more subtle acquired mental sign known as a *nimitta*. The sense of touch (physical sensation of the breath) is shut down and you now experience the breath as a purely mental object, perceived for example as a white light, a blue pearl or perhaps a sensation of rapture. This is like the full moon (the mind) coming out from behind the clouds (the world of the five senses). This subtle object then becomes the focus of your meditation and carries you through the higher attentional stages.

Ajahn Chah likens the emergence of this sign to a shy animal, which would only come close to you if you are absolutely still. Similarly, if you are absolutely still the nimittas come out, and only if you continue to be absolutely still do they remain. Another simile is a dark room, in which you can eventually see shapes as your eyes become accustomed to the darkness. In the same way, the nimitta gradually emerges from the formless stillness once the breath has 'disappeared'.

The next two lines of the sutta instruct us what to do if subtle forms of dullness and excitement arise while you are focused on the nimitta:

Breathing in gladdening the mind,
*   breathing out gladdening the mind*
Breathing in concentrating the mind,
*   breathing out concentrating the mind*

It may be that your experience of the nimitta is dull or stained, perhaps because your mental energy is low. The antidote is to bring more joy into the meditation and experience this mental object more fully. You can focus more intently on the center of the nimitta, sharpen your attention or perhaps return to the previous stage, focusing on the beautiful breath. You can also heighten your joy by recollecting the Three Jewels or recalling the benefits of virtues such as loving kindness.

If, on the other hand, the appearance of the nimitta is unstable, you must ensure that your mind is perfectly still and concentrated. This means not only keeping the image still, but keeping the knower still as well, that aspect of mind which 'sees' the image. When the nimitta first arises you may encounter fear or excitement, just as when you meet a stranger for the first time. In the same way that you learn to relax in this stranger's company as you get to know them, you can learn to loosen the mind a little and stay present with the beautiful nimitta.

There are two attentional stages which correspond to these stages of breathing meditation:

6. *Pacifying the Mind*

Subtle dullness has been overcome during the previous stage (although traces still remain) and there is now a danger of overly invigorating the mind. This leads to the arising of subtle agitation or excitement which needs to be pacified. In this stage mindfulness and vigilance become more intense, being refined through uninterrupted attention, and subtle excitement is thus overcome. You may have a habit of loosening the mind whenever subtle excitement appears; this may be necessary at times, though at this stage you also need to increase your vigilance and tighten the mind in order to overcome it.

In the fifth stage subtle dullness is overcome by the power of *inspired vigilance*, and now during this sixth stage a stronger faculty known as *complete vigilance* is developing. This enables you to overcome subtle excitement though it is not eliminated completely. The quality of attention thus becomes like a clear radio channel, without any extraneous noise or static. As this stage you no longer experience resistance to meditation practice and your sessions may last an hour or more.

7. *Fully Pacifying the Mind*

With inspiration and perseverance, complete vigilance is further developed, so the remaining traces of subtle sinking and excitement are eliminated and therefore vanish completely. You are thus able to abandon subtle sinking and excitement as soon as they are produced through the *power of enthusiastic diligence*. In this way as soon as sinking sets in you arouse your attention, and when excitation occurs you loosen up slightly. These attentional imbalances are thus swiftly recognised and are easily remedied with quite subtle adjustments.

V. Unifying the Mind (Like an Ocean Unmoved by Waves)

The practice of breath awareness has now shifted to awareness of a beautiful stable mental sign, or nimitta. Having overcome almost every trace of dullness and excitement, the meditation is now proceeding smoothly and effortlessly. You learn to trust your experience completely and remain absorbed in the object, trying to relinquish all control as the intense beauty of the nimitta holds your attention without your assistance. You simply enjoy the ride as your attention gets drawn to the center or the light expands and envelops you.

Continuing on with the example of the shy animal which only comes close to you when you are still, you notice that more animals come out when you are even stiller. At first only ordinary animals come out, but now strange and wonderful animals emerge. Similarly, further nimittas come out which carry you to even deeper levels of meditation. In particular, a more subtle mental sign known as the counterpart sign (*patibhaga nimitta*) appears at a certain stage, as if breaking out from the acquired sign. It is far more purified, though it has neither a colour nor shape. The appearance of this sign corresponds to the attainment of shamatha. The final stages of the Buddha's Anapanasati practice refer to the experience of jhana meditation and insight, which are discussed later.

This description is equivalent to the final two attentional states which lead directly to shamatha, the tenth stage:

8. One-Pointedness

At this stage you develop a special spontaneous ability to fix one-pointedly on the object for as long as you wish. A little exertion is required at the beginning of the meditation and then you can flow with the momentum of the practice without interruption and without further exertion. Subtle sinking and excitement are therefore eliminated with a small degree of effort through the power of enthusiastic diligence. In this eighth stage you attain *uninterrupted engagement*, which means the mind can focus with continuous absorption on the object of concentration. This is in contrast to the previous stages which are all achieved with interrupted engagement.

In this stage you can sustain a highly focused attention for about three hours or so, and your mind is still like an ocean unmoved by waves, ruffled only by the occasional ripple.

9. *Equanimity*

At the ninth stage there is an effortless entering into, and abiding in, deep meditation. The mind places itself on the object of its own accord, effortlessly and spontaneously. This is achieved through the power of *complete familiarity* and spontaneous engagement. The mind is now perfectly pacified and the arising of subtle dullness and excitement is not even possible, and you can maintain flawless concentration for at least four hours. However, if you discontinue your practice then dullness and excitement can still erode your state of attentional balance, as they have not been completely eliminated.

Achieving this ninth attentional state is the peak attainment in the 'desire realm', which describes the mental state of human beings. This naturally leads to the attainment of shamatha.

10. *The Attainment of Shamatha*

When shamatha is actually achieved, there is a radical transition in your body and mind and you feel like a butterfly emerging from its coccoon. Your mind at this stage has gone beyond the desire realm and you now have gained access to the *form realm*, a subtle dimension of consciousness that transcends the realm of physical senses.

This shift is characterised by specific experiences that take place in a short space of time. Firstly, a powerful wind enters through your crown and dissolves throughout your body, and you feel as though you have been filled with the power of a blissful dynamic energy. Both your body and mind are now imbued with a special kind of pliancy, making the body feel buoyant and freed from physical dysfunction, and filling the mind with an overwhelming feeling of joy. You have a sense of complete freshness and increased mental capacity - your mind is therefore like an oil lamp not moved by the wind, resting bright and clear, unmoved by anything.

Once you have attained shamatha you can enter this state at will and meditate for as long as you wish without interruption, and you can even survive without basic requirements such as food, drink or sleep. During meditation your attention is completely withdrawn from the physical senses, discursive thoughts and mental images, though you can cue yourself to emerge from meditation after a specified period. However, afflictive tendencies are not completely eradicated and strong emotions may still surface under certain conditions. If, on the other hand, you are able to genuinely renounce worldly concerns and wish to attain freedom from suffering, you can use shamatha as a tool to gain direct insight into the truth of impermanence, suffering and selflessness. This can lead to complete elimination of all afflictive emotions and mental states, since when you realise that no 'self' exists, these states of mind have nothing to hang onto. This is nirvana.

VI. A Summary of the Shamatha Path

Traditionally the nine attentional states leading to shamatha are depicted by a drawing of an elephant, a monkey and a monk, as shown below. Five symbols represent the five sense objects, the objects of agitation to the mind. The black elephant represents coarse mental dullness, the black monkey represents coarse agitation and the monk symbolises the meditator.

*9 Progressive Stages of Mental Development: The Six Powers of Study,
Contemplation, Memory, Comprehension, Diligence and Perfection*

At first the black monkey has complete control of the elephant, meaning that you are naturally controlled by distractions. The monk initially works very hard to try to bring the mind under his control and the fire symbolises the great effort that is required. With persistent effort the monk gradually starts to control the elephant and so with great discipline you begin to overcome agitation. The elephant becomes whiter, which means that coarse dullness is slowly being eradicated though the effort of meditation. However, at this point a small black hare appears on top of the elephant, signifying subtle dullness. Continuing meditation practice diligently, you arrive at the next stage, at which point the monkey has lost control of the elephant but still tries to interrupt occasionally. This means you only have occasional difficulties with agitation and mental dullness.

Gradually the monkey interrupts less and less and the monk gains greater control of the elephant. The elephant becomes whiter until it is completely white. At this point the monkey can no longer control the elephant at all. Finally you reach the stage where your mind has been completely pacified and you can fully control your mind rather than being driven by your emotions. This is shown by the monk meditating while the elephant is completely pacified. Beyond this stage, we see the monk meditating while sitting on the elephant. We also see two rainbow lines emerging from the monk's heart, which symbolise the development of supernatural powers upon mastery of shamatha meditation. You have then gained the ability to focus the single-pointed mind on the development of insight, or vipasyana meditation. Depending on which type of path you are following, you can then progress through various stages of deepening insight until you finally reach enlightenment.

According to the Theravada tradition, accomplishing shamatha using the breath as an object places you at the threshold of experiencing the jhanas, states of concentration which are even more brilliant and powerful, and these lead directly to insight. The Buddha summarised this path by stating that mindfulness of breathing was 'one thing which, when developed and cultivated, would fulfill four things' – the four foundations of mindfulness. These four foundations are described as 'four things which, when cultivated, would fulfill seven things'. These are the *seven factors of enlightenment* - mindfulness, investigation, discrimination, energy, joy, tranquility, concentration and equanimity. These seven factors, then, were described as 'seven things which, when developed and cultivated, would fulfill two things' – true knowledge and liberation.

The texts state that at least six to twelve months of full-time practice are usually required to attain shamatha, yet this varies significantly between individuals. In the Jonang tradition of Tibetan Buddhism one would practise in a dark room with the aim of attaining shamatha, and for the best meditators this would take as little as one hundred days. However, certain preliminaries are usually needed to engage in this tantric practice as it is quite advanced.

CHAPTER 3
The Hindrances to Meditation Practice

Knowing the hindrances to meditation practice is essential in order to understand the current state of your mind and discover how to overcome counterproductive emotions and mental states. The hindrances that emerge during meditation are the same as the hindrances that emerge in daily life, so by learning to overcome them you are developing a very useful skill. Being aware of the hindrances can also help you 'start where you are' and have more realistic expectations of your practice, acknowledging that it takes time to change certain lifelong habits. At a more advanced level, it can help you identify precisely what stage of the meditation path you have reached and how to proceed further.

In the Theravada tradition five hindrances are described - sensual desire, ill will, restlessness and remorse and uncertainty (or doubt). Each of these can be overcome with specific remedies, and they are removed completely at certain advanced stages of meditation. The Mahayana tradition, meanwhile, speaks of five faults in meditation practice which occur in various degrees during the nine attentional states, and these are overcome by applying eight corresponding antidotes. I will first describe the five hindrances and then explain the five faults, together with their antidotes. This is followed by a description of five methods to remove distracting thoughts following the Theravada tradition.

5 Hindrances to Meditation Practice.

I. The Five Hindrances

The five hindrances are gradually weakened and finally removed as you progress along the meditation path. As you begin to meditate and discover how noisy your mind actually is, they may completely dominate your practice. However, as your practice progresses they gradually subside and you discover a mind which is naturally calm and clear.

These five hindrances are:

1. *Sensual Desire*

   This is likened to a still forest pool mixed with coloured clay. If you were to examine your facial reflection in this pool of water, you wouldn't recognise it or see it clearly. Similarly, by dwelling in a mind overwhelmed by sensual desire and not knowing how to escape from this state of mind, you fail to see reality as it is and are unable to benefit yourself or others.

   Sensual desire refers not only to uncontrolled lust, but also to attachment to objects of the five senses – attractive sights, sounds, smells, tastes and tactile sensations. The key to overcoming this hindrance is to abandon it little by little. First you can learn to be mindful and receptive of sense objects without reacting to them, and gradually you will be less inclined to be distracted or 'pulled away' by these objects in meditation and in daily life. Someone with a large amount of sensual desire may also benefit from meditating on the repulsive aspects of the body. It may also help to be aware that the greatest kind of bliss or ecstasy, which we often pursue in sensual desire, can only be found when we *let go* of all desire, as in deep meditation.

2. *Ill Will*

This is likened to a still forest pool which is heated from below, bubbling and boiling. If you were to examine your facial reflection in this pool of water, you wouldn't recognise it or see it clearly. Similarly, by dwelling in a mind obsessed by ill will, you fail to see reality as it is and are unable to benefit yourself or others.

The remedy for ill will is to meditate on loving kindness or metta. Ill will can be directed towards yourself, towards another person or toward the meditation object. Ill will toward oneself is often related to feelings of guilt, unreasonable expectations of oneself or growing up in an environment which lacked compassionate love. It may help to direct loving kindness to the image of a young, innocent child who represents the purity of your true nature. You can counter ill will towards others in a similar way, recalling that everyone is seeking happiness, just like you, and expanding your circle of metta to include those who are both close and distant. Meditation may seem like a chore if you have ill will towards your object, so it can be helpful to view it as a dear friend, learning to love and appreciate it as you would your only child.

3. *Dullness and Drowsiness*

This is likened to a still forest pool covered with moss, algae and slime. If you were to examine your facial reflection in this pool of water, you wouldn't recognise it or see it clearly. Similarly, by dwelling in dullness and drowsiness, you fail to see reality as it is and are unable to benefit yourself or others.

The key to overcoming dullness is to first make peace with it and stop fighting it – otherwise the mind tends to swing wildly between dullness and agitation. If you are in a relaxed state and begin to slip into dullness, it is important to tighten the mind, perking up your alertness as if walking on the edge of a cliff face. You can also reflect on the precious opportunity you have to develop your mind with meditation practice or other inspirational topics. However, if you still feel tired it is best just to rest rather than force the meditation. Sometimes dullness may not be the problem but rather ill will, as we tend to escape into dullness if we don't enjoy what we are doing.

4. *Restlessness and Remorse*

This is likened to a still forest pool stirred by the wind, rippling, swirling and churned into small waves. If you were to examine your facial reflection in this pool of water, you wouldn't recognise it or see it clearly. Similarly, by dwelling in a mind obsessed by restlessness and remorse, you fail to see reality as it is and are unable to benefit yourself or others.

Restlessness is overcome by cultivating an inner sense of contentment, free from expectations and happy to be still and silent. It can also help to loosen up the meditation and ensure the body is relaxed. Remorse is related to an uneasy conscience, and if this is the case it can be counteracted by forgiving yourself and learning from your mistakes, knowing that everyone does make mistakes. More remedies for an agitated state of mind are described later.

5. *Uncertainty or Doubt*

This hindrance arises when you are plagued by indecision, unable to decide on a course of action and see it through. It refers to uncertainty about the Buddha's teachings, the teacher or yourself. It is likened to a still forest pool that is turbid, unsettled and muddy. Again if you were to examine your facial reflection in this pool of water, you wouldn't recognise it or see it clearly. Similarly, by dwelling in a mind overwhelmed by uncertainty, you fail to see reality as it is and are unable to benefit yourself or others.

Uncertainty about the Buddha's teachings can be overcome by examining them and reflecting on the benefits of following them. By studying and practising them, and by seeking encouragement from spiritual friends, you can acquire clarity of mind and faith which is based on reason and direct experience. Uncertainty about the teacher, meanwhile, is overcome by carefully examining them before reaching a conclusion that they are trustworthy. Self-doubt, meanwhile, can be overcome with determination and skilful guidance; you should be aware, however, that this often co-exists with other hindrances such as dullness or ill will towards oneself.

What if, through practice, you are able to overcome these hindrances? This is likened to a still forest pool that is not mixed with coloured clay, not bubbling and boiling, not covered over with moss and slime, not stirred up by the wind and not turbid and muddy, but rather clear, serene and still; then if you were to examine your facial reflection in this pool of water it you would clearly recognise it and see it as it is. So too, when you achieve a state of mind that is no longer obsessed by sensual desire, ill will, dullness and drowsiness, restlessness and remorse or uncertainty, you will see reality as it is and accomplish your own good and the good of others.

II. The Five Faults and the Eight Antidotes

The five faults and eight antidotes provide us with an effective framework to recognise and overcome the hindrances which interfere with our ability to meditate. They describe the different obstacles to successful meditation that emerge as you progress through the nine attentional states leading to shamatha. Knowledge of these faults and their antidotes can help you deal with them as quickly and effectively as possible, not only during meditation but in daily life as well.

The five faults include: laziness, not knowing or forgetting the instructions, mental dullness and agitation, under-application and over-application. The eight antidotes, meanwhile, are: aspiration, faith, diligence, mental pliancy, awareness, mindfulness, application of remedies and equanimity. The five faults, along with their corresponding antidotes, are now described:

1. *Laziness (antidote: aspiration, faith, diligence and mental pliancy)*

    Laziness is a major obstacle to your practice of meditation and also to achieving other goals. Laziness does not only refer to hanging around and doing nothing. There are three types of laziness:

    1.1 *Complacency*

    This manifests as not wanting to meditate or being unwilling to practise, having a lack of desire or disinterest in meditating.

    1.2 *Lack of self-confidence*

    This refers to lack of self-confidence in your ability to meditate and achieve shamatha or any other achievements.

1.3 Being habitually busy

This means occupying yourself with many unnecessary tasks, also known as *active laziness*.

It is vital to be aware of these tendencies. Laziness can be overcome by developing faith in the excellent qualities of meditative concentration and the aspiration to attain these qualities. Only then will we value meditation practice enough to make it a priority in our life. This faith and aspiration inspire us to develop diligence and joyful effort, which eventually bring blissful pliancy and alert ease to the mind. Through the power of familiarity you will achieve both mental and physical pliancy, a unique flexibility of body and mind.

If you become discouraged because you do not feel you are making progress, it can be helpful to recognise the incredible effort we put into other areas of our life such as bringing up children or learning a trade – these often take many years to master. If we really consider the benefits of meditation, we may come to the conclusion that it is worth devoting a similar amount of effort to the task of developing our own minds.

2. *Not Knowing or Forgetting the Instructions (antidote: mindfulness)*

This means your object of meditation or other instructions have not been learnt or have been forgotten, so the mind wanders off to other objects frequently. Changing the object of meditation too often, especially within a single session, is also an obstacle to achieving single-pointed concentration. The remedy for this is mindfulness, which allows you to retain the object of meditation and prevents you from forgetting the instructions. Mindfulness refers both to remembering the meditation instructions and engaging the mind so that it becomes 'full' of the object.

At the same time that you are being mindful, you can also begin to develop vigilance. This means observing the meditating mind itself and detecting when the mind has wandered off the object, even in a subtle way, so you can apply the appropriate remedy. It is like a non-participating commentator reporting on what is happening but not actually joining in.

3. *Mental Dullness and Agitation (antidote: vigilance)*

3.1 *Coarse Agitation:*

During the beginning stages of meditation the mind is agitated and wanders frequently towards external objects. This agitation occurs when your concentration is held too tightly or there is a lot of tension in your body, which is not sufficiently relaxed. As the distracted mind veers off its object of focus completely, this is usually quite easy to detect. In the beginning, however, it may take minutes for the untrained mind to actually notice that the object has been lost. Coarse agitation is likened to the movement of a cloud, which is easy to recognise when it occurs. Applying the remedy is generally not too difficult at this stage.

Remedy

There are various remedies to suit different individuals. You can lower the object, imagine it as heavier, place your tongue against your bottom teeth, close your eyes for a while or concentrate on bodily sensations and make the whole body relax. If the mind is too stimulated and needs to be settled down and subdued, it can also help to meditate on a sobering topic such as the suffering nature of cyclic existence or the imminence of death. Another technique to subdue the mind is to visualise a black dot by your seat. If you are very fidgety, physical exercise will tire you and cause the mind to wander less, as will a heavy, fatty diet. At first wandering thoughts are very difficult to detect, but with time and practise such awareness becomes natural.

3.2 Coarse Dullness

This arises when the mind is cloudy or sleepy and there is no clarity, as the mind is excessively withdrawn inside and on the verge of falling asleep. Here, clarity refers to a clear, fresh and bright state of mind and not to the object of meditation.

Remedy

You can brighten or elevate the meditation object by slightly raising your eyes or paying closer attention to its details, as if you would fall off the edge of a cliff if you lost the object. You can also uplift the mind by recollecting something wholesome or inspiring, such as the qualities of the Three Jewels, or going to an elevated place with a vast view. Another technique to brighten the mind is to imagine a white light at your forehead between your eyes. Staying in a cool and breezy place will also perk up the mind, as will splashing your face with water, exercising outdoors and adhering to a light diet.

You must take great care, however, to distinguish tiredness due to laziness or excessive sleep from tiredness because you genuinely need rest. It also pays to be aware that ill will sometimes manifests as tiredness. If you genuinely need rest you will continue to feel fatigued despite applying the above remedies. In this case it is important to rest, as pushing too hard can be counterproductive.

3.3 Subtle agitation

This is harder to recognise, occurring when part of the mind is comfortably resting on the object of meditation while another part has wandered off to another object without you noticing. This is likened to a quickly moving monkey, which is much harder to detect.

Remedy

To remedy subtle agitation you must develop a particularly strong and powerful vigilance. This cannot be obtained through intellectual means, but only via your own experience and practise. Through the momentum gained with repeated practise, your mind will eventually be able to identify subtle agitation as soon as it arises and return quickly to the object.

3.4 Subtle dullness (sinking)

The fault of subtle dullness, or sinking, is usually not recognised by beginners because they are generally too agitated. It is only recognised when a meditator is more advanced and has the ability to focus on the object with some degree of stability, usually during the fifth attentional state. Subtle dullness occurs when there is fixation and some clarity but no intensity – this means there is little vitality or strength with which the object is being held. This is much harder to detect and eliminate. Many meditators in fact become stuck here, feeling as though their meditation is going very well. This is a common trap.

Remedy

The remedy for subtle sinking is to develop a particularly strong, powerful and vivid intensity, which can only be developed with incredible discipline. This is not something that can be described intellectually but only experienced by skilled practitioners.

It can also help to refresh the mind by reflecting on a topic that inspires you such as gratitude towards your Dharma teacher, the benefits of a precious human birth or the aspiration to reach enlightenment. These thoughts exalt and uplift the mind.

4. *Under-Application (antidote: application of remedies)*

This means not taking enough action to correct dullness, agitation or laziness when they arise. You fail to apply the remedy, often because you are too lethargic or complacent. The remedy here is to take action and apply the relevant antidote. Sometimes it can help to interrupt the meditation by walking around for a while, stretching the body, splashing your face with cool water or getting some fresh air. On returning to your seat you may find it easier to resume your meditation. It can also help to bring to mind the many benefits of meditation practice.

5. *Over-Application (antidote: equanimity)*

This is the mistake of applying remedies when they are not necessary, or applying them excessively. An example might be when sinking and agitation have been recognised and corrected, yet still you continue to apply more corrective action. The antidote to this problem is to apply 'equanimity'. In other words, leave it alone.

If you memorise these five faults and eight antidotes, your meditation will no longer be a 'hit and miss' affair, but rather a dynamic process from which you are sure to benefit. In order to train yourself to recognise these faults and apply the antidotes, it can be helpful at first to deliberately alternate between loosening and sharpening the mind. For example, you may take several deep breaths, saying 'relax' on the out-breath, loosening your posture, placing the tongue under the bottom teeth or visualising a black dot at your perineum, followed by several breaths saying 'alert' with the out-breath, tightening your posture, placing the tongue behind the top teeth or visualising a white dot at your forehead. As you progress your adjustments will become less frequent and more and more subtle, as you learn to swiftly recognise dullness and agitation and gradually develop the skills of mindfulness and vigilance.

III. FIVE WAYS TO REMOVE DISTRACTING THOUGHTS

The Theravada tradition describes five ways to remove distracting thoughts, which are additional remedies for the hindrances to meditation practices. These are highly practical instructions which can help you overcome intrusive thoughts and settle the mind, and are relevant not only to your meditation practice but to daily life as well. The later remedies are generally effective if previous ones have failed. Interestingly, these techniques also encompass many of the techniques which are used in modern psychology.

These five instructions are:

1. *Paying attention to wholesome states of mind*

    If unwholesome thoughts arise connected with desire, hate and delusion, and you give attention to other thoughts which are wholesome, then the unwholesome thoughts subside and are eventually abandoned and the mind becomes steadied, unified and concentrated. This is likened to a skilled carpenter knocking out and extracting a coarse peg by using a fine one.

Two opposed mental processes cannot take place simultaneously, just as fire and water cannot exist at the same time. For example, you cannot feel love and hatred at same instant, and therefore focusing on loving kindness will help you overcome hatred.

2. *Reflecting on the dangers of distracting thoughts*

If unwholesome thoughts still arise you should examine the dangers or disadvantages of such thoughts, thinking, 'They are unwholesome, reprehensible and only result in suffering for myself and others'. In so doing any unwholesome thoughts subside and are eventually abandoned. This is likened to a woman fond of ornaments being disgusted, shocked and humiliated if she sees the carcass of a snake or dog hanging around someone's neck.

Buddha used many examples to point out the dangers of holding onto thoughts and feelings. He once likened these to grass or reeds by the side of a river – though you may think you can hold onto them and climb ashore, they break off and you are carried further down the river. In the West the tradition of *cognitive therapy* challenges us to reflect on the dangers of thinking in a particular way and analyse how we could view things more realistically.

3. *Not giving attention to distracting thoughts*

If unwholesome thoughts still arise you should try to forget these thoughts and not give any attention to them, and in so doing they subside and are eventually abandoned. This is likened to someone with good eyes not wanting to see forms that come within range of sight, therefore shutting their eyes or looking away.

This means that we can train ourselves not to get caught up or fused with painful thoughts and feelings. This does not mean you are avoiding them; rather, they are still there in the periphery of your awareness yet you refuse to buy into them or let them affect how you live. In the West the tradition of *Acceptance and Commitment Therapy* (ACT) has a variety of 'defusion techniques' to lessen the impact of distracting thoughts.

4. *Stilling the thought formations*

If unwholesome thoughts still arise you should give attention to stilling the thought-formation of those thoughts. In so doing any unwholesome thoughts subside and are eventually abandoned. This is likened to a man walking fast thinking, 'Why am I walking fast? What if I walk slowly?' and deciding to walk slowly. Then he might consider, 'Why am I walking slowly? What if I stand?' and he would stand. Then he might consider, 'Why am I standing? What if I sit?' and he would sit. Finally he might consider, 'Why am I sitting? What if I lie down?' and he would lie down. In so doing he would abandon postures that were more coarse in preference for postures that were more subtle. So too, by giving attention to stilling the thought formations, unwholesome thoughts subside and are eventually abandoned.

In the West there are many techniques based on mindfulness and relaxed awareness, helping people gain a calmer mind which is less affected by distracting thoughts.

5. *Crushing the mind with the mind*

If unwholesome thoughts and emotions still arise then the final step is to beat down and 'crush' the mind with the mind, with teeth clenched and tongue pressed against the roof of the mouth. This is likened to a strong man seizing a weaker man by the head and shoulders and beating him down, constraining and crushing him. In this way unwholesome thoughts subside and are eventually abandoned.

This technique is reminiscent of the tantric approach of working with strong emotions. Just as a skilled doctor is able to transform poison into medicine, so too can we learn to simply recognise the raw energy of emotions without attaching a story to them, without suppressing or following them impulsively. For example, instead of letting anger carry you away towards shame or violent action, you can recognise the intense clarity and deep caring at its core. You can stay with this feeling until it dissolves, just like a surfer riding a wave. In the West there are similar techniques to accept or 'release' strong emotions, rather than avoiding them or buying into them.

These five methods to remove distracting thoughts offer a fresh perspective on how to overcome the hindrances to meditation practice, and also how to overcome states of emotional conflict in daily life. Becoming familiar with these techniques can help your meditation practice substantially, especially when strong emotions surface.

CHAPTER 4
Analytical Meditation

I. WHAT IS ANALYTICAL MEDITATION?

While shamatha emphasises calming, unifying and concentrating the mind, the purpose of analytical meditation, or *vipasyana*, is to wake the mind up by examining the nature of our experience. When built on the foundation of a calm mind, this process allows you to bring the many different concepts from Buddhist philosophy together into a single unified understanding. In this way thoroughly investigating and gaining a *conceptual understanding* of these topics builds a foundation for achieving *non-conceptual* or *direct* insight. You can then see directly the Four Noble Truths and the Four Seals. Impermanence, suffering and selflessness are then inside you, part of your experience.

There are many different levels of insight, and each level can be beneficial in helping achieve a more realistic and compassionate view of reality. Only the highest level, however, will lead to the complete eradication of our afflictive emotions and mental states. In order to achieve this, you must have attained an extremely refined level of concentration - at least shamatha. Although momentary concentration may give you brief glimpses or 'flash experiences' of direct insight, especially if you are following a devotional path, this will not be enough to overcome the afflictions unless it is accompanied by a strong and stable mind.

This assertion is supported by the great Mahayana master Shantideva:

> *Realising that one who is well endowed with vipasyana*
> *by way of shamatha eradicates mental afflictions,*
> *one should first seek shamatha.*

Similarly, Asanga states that as soon as shamatha has been achieved, one should focus one's attention single-pointedly inward on the mind. The Theravada tradition agrees that the minimum requirement for true insight (also known as *stream entry*) is the mind of shamatha, as this mind is temporarily free from the hindrances. Greater penetration, however, may be achieved with the even more refined states of concentration of the jhanas.

This does not mean, however, that you should 'defer' analytical meditation until after you have achieved shamatha. First, it is crucial to develop a good conceptual understanding of core Buddhist principles ('right view') such as the Four Noble Truths, two truths and ground, path and result before embarking on the path – this gives you a clear map of how you can arrive at your destination. Second, it is helpful to continually reflect upon and strengthen your motivation for practising the path ('right intention'), contemplating such topics as impermanence and loving kindness – this intention is what determines the result of your practice. Third, a basic understanding of Buddhist wisdom can be of great practical benefit in your daily life – it can help you become less reactive, wiser and closer to others.

The process of analytical meditation, whatever level you engage in it, involves what is known as *three wisdom tools* – first you hear or read a particular teaching, then you study and contemplate it, and thirdly you rest with conviction in its meaning in single-pointed concentration, making it 'part of yourself'. This last step is what we actually mean by meditation, as you have already learned about it and contemplated its meaning, and now you meditate to make it stable in your mind. Therefore you are following a gradual process, first establishing wisdom through hearing followed by wisdom through contemplation, which finally leads to wisdom through meditation.

First I will describe an effective method for analysing any topic of our choice and then I will explore how we can use analytical mediation to understand a variety of topics presented in this book, dealing with both relative and ultimate truth.

II. THE PROCESS OF ANALYTICAL MEDITATION

To transform a particular topic into an object of meditation, you should first formulate it as a question (for example, 'Does the self exist in my body?') and then direct the mind to investigate how this question applies to yourself, in light of all the teachings you have studied. You should continue this until a *feeling* of certainty and clarity arises (for example, that my mind just has habits of identifying with the body on certain occasions, but there is no 'self' in it at all!). Then you can drop the analysis and rest in this feeling of certainty for as long as it lasts, remaining in a more receptive state of mind.

Discursive thoughts will inevitably arise and you can use this as a cue to begin analysis again, either on the same or a different topic, using your thoughts in a controlled way. When once again you experience a sense of certainty and conviction, you rest again, as before. In this way you can alternate between analysis and resting meditation, gradually deepening and refining your understanding so that you will be primed to experience the non-conceptual reality of emptiness.

Jamgon Kongtrul gives some useful guidelines about how to alter between analytical and resting meditation in his *Treasury of Knowledge*:

> *If due to intense analysis the ability to rest deteriorates,*
>> *Do more resting meditation and replenish the stillness.*
> *If due to prolonged resting you no longer want to analyse,*
>> *Do analytical meditation to strengthen the mind's clarity.*

Jamgon Kongtrul

Thus if you find the mind gets agitated by practising analytical meditation, you should allow it to settle once more by relaxing the body and practising single-pointed meditation for a while. On the other hand, if your resting meditation leads to dullness, you can increase your mental clarity by resuming your analysis. Furthermore, when you become accustomed to the process of alternating between analysis and resting, you eventually reach a stage when not so much analysis is needed to give rise to certainty. Thus it is important that you emphasise analysis when you begin with the practice and later on leap quickly into resting meditation once you are more accomplished.

III. Analytical Meditation and the Two Truths

Using the tool of analytical meditation, you can contemplate any subject you choose to direct your mind towards. The Buddhist path is structured in such a way that encourages us to view the relative truth and the ultimate truth as equally important, and therefore you should contemplate both of these, not neglecting one at the expense of the other. The 'relative truth' is to do with the way we see everyday reality, while the 'ultimate truth' is the true nature of this experience. These are like two wings of a bird, and one cannot be fully developed without the other. In the beginning you should emphasise contemplation at the level of relative truth, as this is most relevant to your experience, while later on you can emphasise the ultimate truth more. Enlightenment, then, is when you discover that in reality there is no separation between relative and ultimate truth.

1. Relative Truth

Gaining understanding at the level of relative truth is crucial if you wish to attain enlightenment, since this is what determines your strength of motivation as well as how you act in the world. In particular, you cannot achieve renunciation without deeply contemplating subjects such as impermanence, suffering, karma, the preciousness of human life and the benefits of liberation and taking refuge. If you are aiming for complete enlightenment, it is essential to contemplate and develop bodhicitta, the compassionate wish to lead all beings to liberation, knowing that you can only fulfill this wish by unveiling your own Buddha-nature. Furthermore, if you are following a tantric path then it is crucial to understand the supreme importance of the Dharma teacher and contemplate the meaning of devotion and pure perception, which is an essential preliminary for all tantric practice.

A very useful contemplation for everyone is on the subject of loving kindness or *metta*. With this contemplation you can gain a conviction that all beings are equally worthy of love and compassion, just like yourself. An example of such a contemplation appears in the *Metta Sutta:*

> *May all beings be happy and at ease; may their minds be contented. Whatever living beings there may be – feeble or strong, long (or tall), stout or medium, short, small or large, seen and unseen, those dwelling far or near, those who are born and those who are yet to be born – may all beings, without exception, be happy and at ease!*
>
> *Let not one deceive another nor despise any person whatever in any place. In anger or ill will let not one wish any harm to another. Just as a mother would protect her*

only child even at the risk of her own life, just so let one culti-
vate a boundless heart towards all beings. Let one's thoughts
of boundless love pervade the whole world – above, below
and across – without any obstruction, without any hatred,
without any enmity.

A similar contemplation based on the Tibetan tradition is as
follows:

Begin by recognising that all beings, just like yourself,
are seeking happiness and its causes. Bring to mind someone
close to you, a neutral person and someone you may consid-
er an enemy, and think of how they are all equally seeking
happiness and wanting to avoid suffering. Then focus on the
person who you are close to, remembering their kindness
to you and thinking: I wish they could be happy... if only
they could be happy! Then think of the neutral person: I
wish they could be happy... if only they could be happy!
Then bring to mind your enemy or someone you may have
a grudge against: I wish they could be happy... if only they
could be happy! You may also wish to bring to mind a young
child who symbolises yourself - innocent, pure and worthy
of all the compassionate love in the world: I wish they could
be happy... if only they could be happy!
You can then include others in your contemplation in
they same way that you might add entries to a computer
spreadsheet, extending your loving kindness to your family,
your neighbours, your immediate surroundings, your
country and finally to the whole world, embracing all living
beings without exception. You may also like to combine
this with a visualisation of red or pink light emerging from

a rose at the center of your heart, filling your entire body. You can then extend this light outward to embrace your surroundings, touching all living beings with the light and warmth of loving kindness.

2. Ultimate Truth

Deep analysis of the ultimate truth is the second vital aspect of the Buddhist path, as a correct conceptual understanding of emptiness or selflessness will ensure you never stray from the correct path. As you progress along the path your experience begins to match this understanding, and eventually you can discard your 'conceptual understanding' in the same way that we leave a raft by the river bank once we have reached the other side of a river.

From a Theravada point view there are a variety of approaches or 'doors' to understanding the ultimate truth ('right view'), but the essence of all approaches is the *Three Marks of Existence*: impermanence (*anicca*), suffering (*dukkha*) and selflessness (*anatman*). For example, the five aggregates which make up our body and mind - form, feeling, perception and memory, thought formation and consciousness.- are observed to be impermanent, uncontrollable and insubstantial. The objects of the senses, sense organs, sense consciousnesses and every experience we encounter are also observed to possess these three characteristics. Contemplating the four foundations of mindfulness naturally leads to the realisation of impermanence, suffering and selflessness, as do the final four instructions of Buddha's teaching on *Anapanasati*:

Breathing in aware of impermanence,
   breathing out aware of impermanence
Breathing in aware of fading away,
   breathing out aware of fading away

Breathing in aware of liberation,
  breathing out aware of liberation
Breathing in letting go,
  breathing out letting go.

In the Tibetan tradition there are also a variety of approaches to understanding emptiness, yet they all follow the Madhyamika or Middle Way philosophy. These contemplations lead one to understand not only the selflessness of the person, but also the selflessness and interdependence of all phenomena. In the Gelug tradition the *inseparability of emptiness and dependent arising* is emphasised. Because phenomena lack true existence they appear in a process of dependent arising, and because they are depending arisings, they lack any true or substantial existence. In contrast, the Jonang tradition arrives at the same understanding by analysing of the *three natures*. The basis for the emptiness of the *imputed nature* is the *dependent nature*, and the basis for the emptiness of the dependent nature is the *primordial* or *ultimate nature*.

The Kagyu and Nyingma traditions, meanwhile, emphasise a more direct approach of asking questions in meditation to penetrate the mind's true nature. An abbreviated example of such a contemplation, based on the ninth Karmapa's *Mahamudra* teachings, is as follows:

Look at the nature of mind when it is still or settled and ask: Does it have a colour, form or shape? Does it have an arising, ceasing, an enduring, or not? Is its nature a state of total blankness or is it a clear, vivid brightness?...

Similarly, let a thought or feeling arise and examine its nature: Is there a place it arose from, a place it endured in, or a place it ceased into? Is it located outside or inside the body? Is the nature of the thought or feeling a bright, clear awareness, and is there any difference between this and the bright, clear awareness you saw in the settled mind?...

Then you should examine the mind reflecting appearances and in relation to the body: When reflecting an appearance (form, sound, taste and so forth), are the mind and the appearance two separate things? If not, how are they related? Are the body and mind the same or different?...

Finally, you should examine the nature of the still mind and moving mind together: Do the still mind and moving mind come up alternately? Is the still mind like a field and the moving mind that arises like a crop growing in it? Or are these two the same like a rope and its coils (in that you cannot have a coil separate from the rope)?

In this way you come to understand the nature of mind, or emptiness, by way of *four insights*: the nature of the mind when it is still (removing the subject), the nature of the mind when it is moving (removing the object), the nature of mind in relation to appearances and the body (removing both the subject and the object) and the nature of the still and moving minds together (removing neither the subject nor the object).

A similar approach involving progressive insights is used in the Zen (or Chan) tradition. This is accomplished by the use of *koans* to pierce through the conceptual mind, such as *what was my original face before I was born?*, or *mu* (the answer given by a great Zen master to the question: does a dog have Buddha-nature? Literally it means 'no'). These contemplations cannot be solved by logical reasoning but only by deeper non-conceptual insight, and a student's insights are repeatedly checked by a teacher.

In essence, the tool of analytical meditation allows you to deepen your understanding of both the relative and ultimate truth, and to see how this relates to your own experience. You can gradually see how insight into the relative truth leads to a deeper understanding of ultimate truth, as the greater renunciation and compassion you develop, the more you can appreciate the inter-dependent nature of reality, and the more 'selfless' you become. Conversely, when you appreciate how nothing exists substantially and independently, you gain a profound respect, love and compassion for others.

CHAPTER 5
Advanced Meditation Objects

I. Open Awareness as a Meditation Object

While true insight can certainly be gained through analytical meditation, another approach which some people might prefer is meditation based on *open awareness* or *settling the mind in its natural state*. Like breath awareness, this method is well-suited to those whose minds are prone to agitation or compulsive thinking. However, to engage properly in these practices it is often necessary to have completed certain preliminary practices.

Have accomplished a certain degree of concentration, you can then focus and be mindful of the nature of your own experience without the need for any specific meditation object. In this way you can let the mind release itself from all its habitual patterns and gradually settle in its ground state. This process can be enhanced by opening the eyes and focusing on the empty space in front of you, simply watching and following thoughts, feelings, perceptions, memories and sensations as they arise and dissolve back into this empty space, yet not being caught up in them.

In the Theravada tradition, the *Satipathana Sutta* speaks of mindfulness of phenomena, including the five aggregates, the sense objects and other objects of awareness. One interpretation of this is to let the mind relax into a state of 'unfastened mindfulness', simply watching the mind as objects arise and dissolve back into the state of open awareness. In the Zen tradition there is a similar practice known as *shikan-taza,* which often complements the use of koans as a meditation object.

In the Tibetan tradition there are a variety of meditation techniques which use open awareness as an object. A text from the Kagyu tradition offers the following instruction to deal with thoughts that arise:

> *No matter what thoughts arise, just recognise them for what they are, placing your attention right upon them without thinking 'I must block them', or feeling happy or unhappy. Just look at them with the eye of discriminating awareness, recognising that they are merely the play of the mind and letting them pass without grasping... like a parade of characters marching across a stage.*

In the Nyingma tradition this is sometimes known as *stillness, movement and awareness* and the instruction is as follows:

> *Recognise movement while remaining in stillness,*
> *When movement occurs, hold the ground of stillness,*
> *When there is no longer any distinction*
> *between stillness and movement,*
> *That is the introduction to one-pointedness.*

Therefore whenever movement arises you should not freeze the stillness or obstruct the movement – instead recognise the movement immediately as it arises. Then, by simply recognising the movement while holding the ground of stillness, the movement will dissolve back into the stillness. Eventually you can reach a vibrant stage in which movement can occur within the stillness and stillness can happen during the movement, as the movement does not produce any distraction.

The state of mind achieved with this practice is characterised by three qualities: bliss, luminosity and non-conceptuality. This mind is like the sky, vast and spacious. Whatever moves through it, whether this be clouds, rainbows or lightning, the sky doesn't react. Like the sky, you can train yourself to be attentive to everything that comes up in the mind without grasping onto anything. Continuing this practice can lead to shamatha and then direct insight as you gradually discover the three qualities of the enlightened mind – its empty essence, cognisant nature and all-pervasive compassion.

In the Jonang tradition, the state of non-conceptual open awareness is the focus of the dark room tantric shamatha practice. The special posture, with the eyes wide open gazing into the darkness at the level of the forehead, is a very effective tantric method to 'force' the mind into the non-conceptual state and use this as an object for single-pointed concentration. Unlike the methods of most other traditions, no process of 'questioning the mind's nature' is necessary. This is an extraordinary method which highlights the subtle, profound and unique features of the tantric path.

A final comment is that the practice of open awareness (or any meditation practice) can be enhanced by spending some time after the meditation recollecting what experiences you went through. You can either jot down your experiences in a journal, discuss them with a partner or simply spend several minutes recalling how your mediation went, including the thoughts, emotions, associations, sensory experiences, mental images and memories you encountered. This kind of *recollective awareness* can greatly enhance your ability to maintain awareness throughout your meditation practice.

II. The Jhanas as a Meditation Object

The jhanas are extremely refined, blissful and completely absorbed states of mind which you can experience after attaining shamatha. There are eight jhanas altogether which are attained in sequence, made up of four *form jhanas* (where a subtle type of form is present) and four *formless jhanas*, where there are no boundaries to one's awareness and the perception of any kind of form has vanished. Entering these states requires a complete surrender of control, and the length of time you spend in these states depends on the 'momentum' of concentration that you have established. The four form jhanas can take you to deeper states of concentration than shamatha and can therefore help you develop insight, while the four formless jhanas are generally not so useful.

Entrance to the jhanas is described in the twelfth stage of the Anapanasati sutta:

> *Breathing in liberating the mind,*
> *breathing out liberating the mind*

According to this instruction, entering a jhana is a process of completely freeing the mind which involves sinking or diving into the subtle mental object that is the focus of your meditation. Alternatively, brilliant light may envelop you along with a feeling of rapture, as you enter a state which is completely blissful but fully mindful and stable. While absorbed in this state you do not have any sense of spatial location, including what is happening with your body, nor can you hear, see or say anything.

According to Buddhism, the jhana states equate to the experience of the *form* and *formless* realms, where beings are said to be reborn if they familiarise themselves strongly with these meditation experiences or become attached to them. However, if you are not attached to these experiences and approach the practice with the correct view and intention, the jhanas can be an extraordinary meditation object. In particular, the fourth form jhana can help you acquire exceptional single-pointed concentration, and after this experience you can easily penetrate the truth of impermanence, suffering and selflessness.

The mind attained through shamatha practice is a type of form realm mind, described as a preliminary or access state to the realisation of the first jhana. After this has been accomplished, the first of the jhanas is attained through seven preliminary stages after shamatha. Each of the four form jhanas has seven preliminaries stages, known as the seven placements of attention, and they can only be achieved by progressing through these stages sequentially. The descriptions that follow are only approximate explanations, as they describe very subtle states or qualities of mind that can be achieved once shamatha is experienced; more detailed descriptions are available but are beyond the scope of this book (in fact Tibetan monks traditionally spend many years studying this topic)

These seven placements of attention are:

1. *Initial Attention*
   In this stage you have the specific attention to initiate the connection with the jhana state.

2. *Discerning Attention*
   This stage has a strong power of discrimination, based on the integration of study and reflection.

3. *Attention arisen from Belief*
   The mind now attains a special quality of conviction.

4. *Isolated Attention*
   At this stage the mind has attention which is totally free of subtle distractions.

5. *Attention of Joy or Withdrawal*
   The quality of this mind is to invite joy within oneself and to experience overwhelming joy.

6. *Analytical Attention*
   The quality of mind at this stage is to have subtle investigation and understanding.

7. *Final Integrating Attention*
   This final stage represents the completion of the qualities reaching toward the actual jhana state of mind.

After emerging from meditation on one of the jhana states, you can recognise the particular jhana by identifying a specific set of qualities. These qualities describe a state of mind that becomes progressively more subtle and act as antidotes to the five hindrances – lethargy, uncertainty, ill will, restlessness and remorse and sensual desire. Although I am describing these qualities with certain words, they are much more subtle and supreme than what these words would normally indicate. The first jhana has four qualities: investigation and analysis, joy, bliss and one-pointedness. On reaching the second jhana, the first quality ceases, so one is left with a mind resting in a state of joy, bliss and one-pointedness. The third jhana is characterised by a state of bliss and one-pointedness, while in the fourth jhana only one-pointedness or equanimity remains. One's concentration is most refined in the fourth jhana and is therefore incredibly powerful.

Beyond the fourth of the form jhanas, a meditator can experience the four formless jhana states: limitless space, limitless consciousness, nothingness and beyond perception. These states are generally not so beneficial, however, as one's state of mind is extremely subtle and lacks the concentration developed in the preceding jhanas. The second of these states, infinite consciousness, can in some cases act as a springboard for the realisation of emptiness, though the other states are generally a hindrance to developing true wisdom. This quality of mind in the formless jhanas has almost no perception, being just a form or subtle experience of mind, and it may project the meditator to a rebirth in the formless realms where no physical forms are experienced: no sound, no smell, no taste and no sensation.

Having already attained shamatha, you have the ability to see that the first jhana is much more subtle than the shamatha mind itself. Perceiving the subtle and peaceful nature of this mind, you are inspired to practise further with diligence in order to achieve the finer levels of the form realm jhanas. Once absorption in the first jhana is achieved, you are inspired to access and absorb yourself in the second, third and fourth jhanas. After emerging from these states, a high degree of stability and vividness is carried over as you engage in your daily activities, when your mind returns to the desire realm. While in meditation you temporarily abandon the afflictive thoughts and emotions which characterise the desire realm; between sessions they still occur, yet with less frequency, intensity and duration.

The powerful concentration achieved in the jhanas also opens up the door towards the attainment of clairvoyance and supernatural powers. By directing the mind to the recollection of past lives, one can attain direct perception of many previous existences, rec-ollecting the nature of one's experience in each of them. One can also develop the 'divine eye', which sees directly the passing away and rebirth of beings and how they move through various realms of existence based on their actions. In addition, one can develop divine hearing, knowledge of the mind of others and supernatural abilities which enable one to control the four elements, such as moving through solid objects, walking on water or flying though space. However, developing these five types of extrasensory abilities does not mean that you have achieved liberation.

Attainment of the various jhanas can lead to rebirth in the various form and formless realms. However, Buddhist meditators generally do not seek rebirth here as it is not usually possible to practise the Buddha's path. Birth in these realms is free from coarse suffering, but like all things this kind of existence must eventually come to an end. Since this is not necessarily the best place to practise, such a birth can be a waste of positive karma. There are, however, exceptional cases of some Buddhist practitioners seeking rebirth in these realms in order to quickly and temporarily pacify afflictions, though complete eradication of their propensities must occur later on. There is also a stage of attainment in the Theravada path known as non-returner, after which one is spontaneously reborn in a form realm before attaining nirvana.

References

Many of the practices touched on in this text can be read about in a more extensive manner in the following books:

Bikkhu Bodhi (ed). *In the Buddha's Words: An Anthology of Discourses from the Pali Canon* (Boston: Wisdom 2005).

John Barter. *Mindfulness Meditations with John Barter.* 2 CD Set. (Sydney 2009).

Ajahn Brahm. *Mindfulness, Bliss and Beyond: A Meditator's Handbook* (Somerville: Wisdom 2006).

Ajahn Chah. *A Still Forest Pool: The Insight Meditation of Ajahn Chah.* Compiled by Jack Kornfield and Paul Breiter (New York: Quest, 1986).

His Holiness the Dalai Lama. *How to See Yourself As You Really Are: A Practical Guide to Self-Knowledge* (London: Rider, 2006).

The Ninth Karmapa Wangchuk Dorje. *The Mahamudra: Eliminating the Ignorance of Darkness.* (Dharamsala: Library of Tibetan Works and Archives, 2002).

Shar Khentrul Jamphel Lodro. *Unveiling Your Sacred Truth through the Kalachakra Path, Books One to Three.* (Melbourne: Tibetan Buddhist Rime Institute, 2016).

B. Alan Wallace. *The Attention Revolution: Unlocking the Power of the Focused Mind* (Boston: Wisdom 2006).

About the Author

Khentrul Rinpoché Jamphel Lodrö is the founder and spiritual director of Dzokden. Rinpoche is the author of many books including Unveiling Your Sacred Truth, The Great Middle Way: Clarifying the Jonang View of Other-Emptiness, A Happier Life, and The Hidden Treasure of the Profound Path.

Rinpoche spent the first 20 years of his life herding yak and chanting mantras on the plateaus of Tibet. Inspired by the bodhisattvas, he left his family to study in a variety of monasteries under the guidance of over twenty-five masters in all the Tibetan Buddhist traditions. Due to his non-sectarian approach, he earned himself the title of Rimé (unbiased) Master and was identified as the reincarnation of the famous Kalachakra Master Ngawang Chözin Gyatso. While at the core of his teachings is the recognition that there is great value in the diversity of all spiritual traditions found in this world; he focuses on the Jonang-Shambhala tradition. Kalachakra (wheel of time) teachings handed down from the Kalki Kings of Shambhala, contain profound methods to harmonize our external environment with the inner world of body and mind. This tantra is connected directly to the Karma of our earth to bring about the Golden age of Peace and Harmony (Dzokden). Khentrul Rinpoche has made it his life mission to spread these precious teachings in as many languages as possible globally so that we can truly transform our world, one person at a time from their inside out.

Rinpoche's Vision

Dzokden was founded with the express purpose of supporting Khentrul Rinpoche in realizing his vision to bring about the Golden Age of peace and harmony in this world. As our community continues to grow and develop, more and more people are getting involved with this extraordinary effort.

To give you a sense of the scope of Rinpoche's vision, we can speak of eight goals that reflect Rinpoche's short and long term priorities:

IMMEDIATE GOALS

Ultimately speaking, lasting, genuine happiness is only possible through profound personal transformation. Now more than ever, we need methods to develop our wisdom and actualise our greatest potential. It is for this reason that Rinpoche places such a heavy priority on the preservation of the Jonang Kalachakra Lineage. There are four ways in which Rinpoche proposes to do this:

1. **Create opportunities to connect with an authentic and complete Kalachakra lineage in close collaboration with dedicated meditators in remote Tibet.** Our goal is to create all of the supports for practicing Kalachakra in accordance with the authentic lineage masters who have upheld this tradition for thousands of years. We do this by commissioning statues and paintings, writing books and giving teachings around the world. We place particular emphasis on ensuring the authenticity of our materials, drawing on the profound experience of highly realised meditators who are dedicating their lives to these practices.

2. **Establish international retreat centres for the study and practice of Kalachakra.** In order to integrate the teachings into our minds, it is crucial to have the opportunity to engage in periods of intensive practice. Therefore, we are working to create the necessary infrastructure that will support and nurture the members of our community to engage in both short and long-term retreat. This includes the purchase of land and the construction of everything that is needed to conduct group and solitary retreats. Our long-term aim is to develop a network of such centres around the world, forming a global community that supports a wide variety of practitioners.

3. **Translate and publish the unique and rare texts of Kalachakra masters.** The Kalachakra System has been the subject of countless texts over the course of Tibet's long history. So far, only a small fraction of these texts have been translated and made accessible in the West. While the theoretical texts are important, we aim to focus particularly on the pith instructions that will guide dedicated practitioners to a deeper experience of these profound teachings.

4. **Develop the tools and programs for a structured learning experience.** With pockets of students distributed throughout the world, we believe it is important to make the most of modern technologies to facilitate the process of learning for our students. Our aim is to develop a robust online educational platform that allows our international community to access quality study programs that are intuitive, structured and engaging.

Long-Term Goals

While we each work towards achieving ultimate peace and harmony in our own minds, we must not lose sight of the fact that we exist within the context of a world filled with a great diversity of individuals. These individuals give rise to a wide variety of beliefs and practices that in turn shape how we relate and interact with each other. In this interdependent reality, it is vital to find viable strategies for promoting greater tolerance and respect. To this end, Rinpoche proposes four specific areas of activity:

1. **Promote the development of a Rimé Philosophy through dialogue with other traditions.** With the desire to be constructive members of a pluralistic society, we need to learn ways of reconciling our differences. To this end, we aim to help people develop the positive qualities that promote an attitude of mutual respect, openness to new ideas and an inquisitive desire to overcome our ignorance.

2. **Develop highly realised role models by offering financial support to dedicated practitioners.** In order to ensure the authenticity of our spiritual traditions, it is imperative that there are people who actualise the highest of realisations. Therefore, we aim to create a financial scholarship program which facilitates genuine practitioners who wish to dedicate their lives to spiritual development, regardless of their system of practice. By helping people actualise the teachings, they become positive role models for those around them, inspiring and guiding the generations to come.

3. **Actualise the great potential of female practitioners by developing specialised training programs.** The Tibetan culture has a long history of cultivating highly realised masters through the intensive training of those who are recognised

to have great potential. Unfortunately, all too often the search for potential was focused only on male candidates. Rinpoche believes that it is increasingly important to have strong, highly realised, female role models who can help to bring greater balance into our world. For this reason, we are working to develop a unique training program for providing women with the opportunity to actualise their spiritual potential. It is our aim to design a specialised curriculum as well as the financial infrastructure to fully support all aspects of their education.

4. **Promote greater flexibility of mind and a broader under-standing of reality through modern educational programs.** In a world that is rapidly evolving, we need to rethink the types of skills that we are teaching our children. The rigid structures of the past are often ill equipped to prepare students for the challenges that they will face during their lives. Therefore, we aim to develop a variety of educational programs that can help children to become more flexible and more capable of adapting to their context. An important part of these programs is the development of greater awareness of the role that our mind plays in our day-to-day experiences. We also aim to bring reforms into the monastic education system that would help make them more relevant for this modern world.

How can you offer your support?

The above will not be possible without your support and participation. A vision of this magnitude requires a great deal of merit and generosity from many benefactors over many years. If you would like to offer your support, please do not hesitate to contact us.

Dzokden
3436 Divisadero Street
San Francisco, California 94123
United States of America
www.dzokden.org

www.ingramcontent.com/pod-product-compliance
Lightning Source LLC
Chambersburg PA
CBHW071209120626
46546CB00006B/2479